Mom

A lifetime of teaching and
making the world a better place

1932–2017

Roadmap for Reading Instruction

How to Help Students Make Great Gains in Reading

Roadmap for Reading Instruction

How to Help Students Make Great Gains in Reading

Practical guidance for
parents,
classroom teachers,
and
reading interventionists

For more information about
Roadmap for Reading Instruction,
plus free content, resources, and videos, visit

http://RIRoadmap.com

(c) 2017, David Bowman
Audacious Leaderrs

978-0-9885078-6-9

No part of this book may be reproduced or transmitted in any form or by any means, electronic or mechanical, including photocopying, recording, or by any information storage and retrieval system, without written permission from the author, of any contributed content herein. Permission is granted for the inclusion of brief quotations in a review.

Printed in the United States of America

Contents

Preface: Getting Great Results — 9

Chapter 1: Environment for Learning — 1

Chapter 2: Principles of Reading Instruction — 9

Chapter 3: Defining the Six Components of Reading — 19

Chapter 4: Oral Language Development — 23
    Breaking Down Oral Language Skills — 25
    What Works for Oral Language Instruction — 29
    What Does Not Work for Oral Language Instruction — 37
    Companion Reading Components — 38

Chapter 5: Phonemic Awareness — 41
    Breaking Down Phonemic Awareness Skills — 43
    Principles for Phonemic Awareness Instruction — 45
    What Works for Phonemic Awareness Instruction — 51
    What Does Not Work for Phonemic Awareness Instruction — 56
    Companion Reading Components — 58

Chapter 6: Phonics — 61
    Breaking Down Phonics Skills — 61
    Principles for Phonics Instruction — 64
    What Works for Phonics Instruction — 68
    What Does Not Work for Phonics Instruction — 72
    Companion Reading Components — 74

Chapter 7: Fluency — 75
    Principles for Fluency Instruction — 78
    What Works for Fluency Instruction — 80
    What Does Not Work for Fluency Instruction — 84
    Companion Reading Components — 85

Chapter 8: Vocabulary — 87
    Breaking Down Vocabulary Skills — 87
    Principles for Vocabulary Instruction — 93
    What Works for Vocabulary Instruction — 97
    What Does Not Work for Vocabulary Instruction — 104
    Companion Reading Components — 105

Chapter 9: Comprehension — 107
    Breaking Down Comprehension Skills — 109
    Principles for Comprehension Instruction — 113
    What Works for Comprehension Instruction — 117

What Does Not Work for Comprehension Instruction	130
Companion Reading Components	132

Chapter 10: The Love of Reading — 133

Appendix A: Description of the Sample Activities	137
Oral Language Development Activities	137
Phonemic Awareness Activities	140
Phonics Activities	143
Fluency Activities	145
Vocabulary Activities	147
Comprehension Activities	149

Appendix B: Sample Lesson Plans	155
K–1 Grade: Green Eggs and Ham	156
2nd–3rd Grade: *Magic Tree House* Series	159
3rd–4th Grade: Spiderman Comics	162
4th–5th Grade: Go for the Gold Series	165
4th–5th Grade: *Island of the Blue Dolphins*	169
6th–7th Grade: Weather Maps	172

Appendix C: Suggested Readings — 175

Preface
Getting Great Results

Six Skills

To read well, students only need to learn six skills. They are

- Oral Language,
- Phonemic Awareness,
- Phonics,
- Fluency,
- Vocabulary, and
- Comprehension.

Each of these skills has several components, and they get more challenging as students get older. But, really, that is all they need to learn. I will walk you through each skill, help you understand what it is and what it looks like in practice, and then I will show you how to help children learn them.

If you create the right environment for learning, if you provide weekly instruction in these skills, if you use proven strategies to help students learn them, and if you address students' interests and reading levels, you will help your students make huge gains in their reading ability. All of that is in this book!

During the last three years, my colleagues and I at the Three Rivers Education Foundation put this theory to the test. We ran a reading intervention program that served more than 17,000 students in grades Kindergarten through 12th grade. Using a small-group format, our reading tutors provided up to 32 hours of instruction over one school semester, about 16 weeks. They conducted two sessions per week, each roughly 45 minutes to 1-1/2 hours long. All students took a pretest and posttest that determined their reading grade level.

Basically, we ran a program that used the conclusions of the National Reading Panel. The panel members looked at the research, and we put their findings into practice. Then we studied our results. And what did we learn from our results?

First, students made gains that far, far exceeded their prior growth. We looked at how much growth students were making before they began our program. It was pretty low, especially compared to the progress they made when we served them. Following the approach in this book, students made about four times the growth than before we served them.

Second, students who received weekly instruction in all six skills did better than students who did not. Same number of instructional hours. Same session lengths. Same types of instructional activities. Very different results.

- **1.53 grade-level increase:** students who received instruction in all six skills every week

- **0.68 grade-level increase:** students who did not receive instruction in all six skills every week

Actually, most teachers would be pretty happy if their students made 0.68 grade-level increases in one semester, which is more than a 1/2-year growth in less than 1/2 year. But what if those students could make more than twice the growth in the same time? Even better!

The results for grades Kindergarten through 5th grade looked like this:

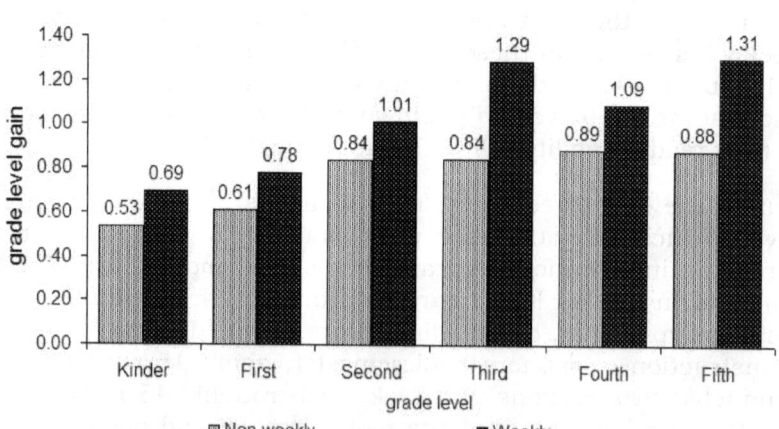

All of the tutors provided instruction in all six skills (some every week and some not), and they all used instructional strategies you will find in this book. That's why even the "non-compliant" tutors got better than expected results.

Once the state assessment results were available, we compared the results for third-grade students in tutors' and non-tutors' classrooms in four diverse districts. Without including results for students who had received tutoring, students in tutors' classrooms significantly outperformed their peers on the English Language Arts assessment. What this means is that the approach in this book works in classrooms, too.

Were the tutors top teachers? No. Most were classroom teachers, many were teachers' aids (education assistants), and the smallest percentage was reading specialists. I am sure some of the teachers were great teachers, and I am equally sure that some were average performers.

Were the students the top students? No. They were in the program for a reason. Overall, about 2% or 3% were on grade level at the beginning, but the rest were behind the grade-level expectations. On average, students began about 2 grade levels behind. Younger students not as much, and older students much, much more.

So how did we manage to get those amazing results? And how can you help students make similar huge gains in reading?

That is what this book will teach you.

Chapter 1
Environment for Learning

For students to make maximum growth in reading, they need the right environment for learning. The three keys to creating the conditions for reading progress are as follows:

1. Create a safe environment,
2. Organize students into groups of three or four students, and
3. Dedicate sufficient time.

This chapter will discuss each of these conditions, with some specific advice for classroom teachers, reading specialists / interventionists, and homeschool teachers.

Create a safe environment.

Before we can talk about reading, we have to think about brains. For learning to occur, the frontal lobes of the brain have to be engaged. Learning requires the neocortex to be active, all the twisty parts on the outside of the brain where we learn, process, interpret, predict, and reason. That is where learning and higher-level processing occur.

However, when we feel threatened, our brains rely on our "reptilian" brain and, to a lesser degree, on our "mammalian brain" and not on our neocortex and frontal lobes. The reptilian and mammalian parts of our brain are where we get anger, fear, avoidance, and attack impulses. When people feel threatened, those parts of the brain become active, causing an automatic fight, flight, or freeze response. It is a survival instinct, but it prevents learning.

Students do not learn when they feel threatened because the "wrong" part of their brain is active. They might learn from the experience later, but when in that survival mode, they are not learning.

What this means for you as the teacher is that your first and most important responsibility is to create an environment in which students feel safe—an environment in which the frontal lobes and not the reptilian brain are activated.

Can all children learn? Yes, but not when they feel threatened or afraid. Think about the struggling readers you know. If they feel threatened, they may engage in fight, flight, or freeze behavior, which is a good indication that they are not learning—and are not capable of learning—at that time.

Fight: aggressive behavior, name calling or insults of other children (or the teacher), throwing things, etc.

Flight: statements that reading is too hard, intentional wrong answers, skipping class or school, going off-task, etc.

Freeze: refusal to participate or respond, keeping quiet, hiding at the back of the classroom, putting one's head on the desk, etc.

Think about how you interact with struggling students and the language you use when talking to students. For example, students will feel threatened if they

- expect insults (e.g., "What's wrong with you? You should know this already!"),

- expect an attack (e.g., "Do it right this time!"),

- anticipate punishment for errors (e.g., "If you keep messing up, you won't get recess!"), or

- believe they will be singled out for their shortcomings (e.g., "Read this aloud to the class").

These beliefs and expectations develop over time following a pattern of interactions with teachers and others. Changing them will also take time and a consistent pattern of positive interactions.

When students learn that correction is not punishment (e.g., "This part is tricky! Here's something we can do to study it in a different way."), they lose the fear of making mistakes. When students expect support (e.g., "Let's try this again. I believe you can do this if we practice it."), they will learn that they are capable of meeting expectations. If they understand that every situation is not a do-or-die, life-threatening scenario ("Sometimes, I have to read things more than once. Which words are you finding confusing? We can figure them out and see if that helps you make sense of this text."), they will learn that you expect improvement, not perfection, that mistakes are acceptable, and that they can keep trying until they get it right.

Ultimately, they will learn that you will provide help and support.

Instead of being in conflict, the students will perceive that you are on their side as they face the challenge of learning to read. Although they may still make mistakes, they believe they will not fail.

You can correct errors, encourage students, and assess their performance without provoking the fight, flight, or freeze responses. As a result, students will realize that your role is to help them learn this necessary skill.

One of your first responsibilities, therefore, is to develop a positive, collaborative relationship with the students. I will discuss this a bit more in the next chapter. When students have positive feelings about the student–teacher relationship, they will be more comfortable taking risks and being vulnerable because they recognize that you care about them. We have seen the power of this relationship in several ways.

First, I have letters and other evidence from students and parents stating, basically, that the students really enjoy receiving tutoring because they enjoy working with the teacher. This is an important distinction. They like doing the hard work of learning to read because of the positive relationship with the tutor. Success does not create a positive relationship. Rather, the relationship leads to success.

Second, education assistants who serve as tutors generally have very good results with students. On the one hand, they typically implement the reading instructional model as it is designed. On the other hand, education assistants are good, often really good, at establishing those positive, supportive relationships with students.

For classroom teachers: Sometimes, you have to discipline students. Kids are kids, and you are the teacher. It is going to happen. Sometimes, too, personalities clash. Sometimes, you have to give low grades. Sometimes. . . . All this together means that reading instruction may be weighed down by prior baggage. This is one reason why we generally did not want classroom teachers to serve as tutors to their students. The most important reason was to give students a different set of instructional opportunities than they receive in the classroom.

If you have had prior conflicts with a student, focus on the goal, and ask the students to do the same. "Now," you say, "we are going to work on helping you be a great reader. That's all that we are going to think about, and I am going to help you. Together, we can do it!" If need be, think about "re-setting" the relationship with the students. Take the time to build a positive relationship. It will pay off when you start to refocus on instruction.

For the reading interventionists: Unless you have been working with a student for a while, you have a fresh start. Before diving into reading, take some time and get to know the students. Talk about interests (see the next chapter), what the student thinks about reading and school, etc. Let them get to know you, too!

On the other hand, if you have been working with the students for while, think about the relationship. On a few occasions, we have had to ask a tutor to pause instruction for a session and just work on the relationship. It paid off. Attendance improved, student participation improved, and the students made good gains in their reading abilities.

For homeschool teachers: So many factors affect the nature of your relationship with your children. When you are the teacher, though, you are the teacher, not just the parent. The challenge that you face is to separate your responsibilities as a parent and as a teacher. Similarly, you have the challenge of separating your relationship as a parent and as a teacher. This may seem difficult to do, but if your goal is improved reading ability, then you need to think about how the relationship affects your students (your children) as they work to improve their reading abilities.

Communicate with your students that other experiences and feelings, other factors of the home life, are not relevant to the time you spend with your students in reading instruction—and you need to model this. Except in one case, that is: you probably have a lot of insights about your students' interests, ability levels, and reading achievements and struggles. This knowledge is immensely valuable as you plan out instructional activities for your children. (See the next chapter for more on this.)

The bottom line: A positive, collaborative relationship with the students is necessary for maximum reading growth. Not only does it allow you to engage students in learning activities as willing participants but also it helps you create the safe environment that students need for learning.

I am not talking about creating a false sense of accomplishment. "Feel good" education does not work. Students' self-esteem will increase when they accomplish something challenging and important, including reading. A supportive environment makes this possible. As students increase their reading ability, their self-esteem will increase—not the other way around. We see this over and over and over. I have many testimonies and letters from teachers, parents, and even students, that students are more confident, more willing to participate in class, and more likely to read on their own. They are not "super readers" yet, but their reading abilities are increasing, and they know it. Instead of perceiving a threat, they see a challenge that, with the support of teachers and peers, they can overcome.

Student grouping is also important for creating a sense of safety and support, but I will address this issue more deeply in the next section.

Organize students into groups of three or four.

The research and our experiences indicate that this is the best group size for teaching reading. And this makes a lot of sense. The best learning activities are based on cooperative learning principles, which means there have to be several students in a group. On the other hand, if more than four students are working in a group, those same activities will leave out some students or, at least, reduce students' need to fully participate.

The students do not have to be at the same reading level. They do need to be fairly close, say within a grade level. One value of the small group setting is that all students in the group can provide valuable input into the process and can learn from each other.

The more advanced students can learn from the less advanced students in a small group. For example, when working on comprehension skills, students may discuss a variety of questions about the text. Once students have a basic understanding of the content, they can discuss responses to those questions whether they are stronger readers or not, and each student lends a unique perspective to help develop greater understanding among all students.

The final reason for small groups refers to the learning climate: a safe environment for participating, making mistakes, trying new skills, and getting support. Students in small groups are not alone. They are not the only ones who are having difficulty with reading. They do not get singled out as less capable than their peers: their peers are right there with them in the reading group.

For classroom teachers: Most likely, you have more than four students in your classroom. You can not ignore the rest of your students in order to work with a single group of three or four students. On the other hand, you can restructure your students to work in various learning stations, participate in small groups, and collaboratively engage in reading activities. You may need to work with the class as a whole to learn how to engage in the various activities, but then student groups can work semi-autonomously while you monitor and provide support as needed.

Or, you can work intently with one group of students while the rest are engaged in other types of cooperative or independent lessons. Think creatively about how you design your learning experiences so that students can work in this optimal group size.

For reading interventionists: In many cases, reading interventionists work one-on-one with students who are struggling to read. Those students are pulled, one at a time, out of their regular classrooms and taken to another place where the reading specialist provides intense support for twenty or thirty minutes.

First, think about this approach from a student's perspective. Conducting reading intervention this way tells the student, "You are not as smart as the rest of your friends. You don't deserve to be with the rest of your classmates." From the onset, pull-out intervention creates an emotional barrier to learning. The student does not want to be singled out from his or her classmates and put into a foreign environment that does not have the comfort and security of a classroom full of peers and friends. It may even seem like a form of punishment.

Of course, this is not the intention. Reading interventionists know that many students struggle with reading, but the student only knows that he or she needs extra help. If a student is pulled out of class as part of a small group, however, the student will recognize that he or she is not alone in struggling to read better. There is safety and a sense of camaraderie that allows learning to occur.

Second, as mentioned above, the most effective reading activities are conducted in groups of three or four. So there is that reason for small-group intervention, too.

For homeschool teachers: If you have one child, then that is what you have, and you go with it. If you have more than one, even at different ages, you have a bit more flexibility. The older children can help the younger children, which strengthens all their reading abilities. On the other hand, and if it is possible, work with other homeschool parents / teachers to bring children together to make the optimal group size of three or four students. This is a tricky one for homeschool parents, but it will produce the best gains in reading ability.

Dedicate sufficient time.

Our best results occurred when students received at least two sessions of reading instruction per week, for around an hour each time.

We did have students who received half-hour sessions three or four times per week, and other students who received less frequent but longer sessions. In both cases, they did not make as much reading progress as students who received instruction twice per week in sessions that lasted from 45 minutes to 1 hour and 15 minutes.

We also had students who received the full 32 hours of instruction in only a month or two. These students, too, did not make the best gains in reading.

Based on our data, students make better reading progress when they receive reading instruction with the following conditions:

- Multiple instructional sessions per week (I do not see any reason not to have three or four sessions per week, time permitting, if the other conditions can be met);
- Sessions that are long enough to engage in meaningful learning activities that address all six reading components (expect to spend at least 45 minutes per session);
- Sessions that are short enough that they do not produce learning burn-out (generally less than one and a half hours);
- Reading instruction over a longer time period; and
- Instructional time dedicated to nothing but reading.

Strong reading skills are necessary for learning all other content areas, and reading instruction needs to be a top priority. Again, think about the brain and the learning process. Simply, brains need enough input, exposure, and time to process the information, make new connections, and develop new skills. You can't rush it. You just have to keep at it.

Chapter 2
Principles of Reading Instruction

The overarching principle of reading instruction (actually, all instruction) is to meet the students where they are. What this means is to tailor the learning experience to the individual child, to recognize how students differ, and to modify the instruction according to what will work for each student. Each student is unique. Here are a few ways that students differ:

- ability in the various reading components,
- interests and hobbies,
- prior experiences (both in school and out of school),
- expectations of self and teachers,
- relationships with others, and
- attitudes about reading and learning.

When instruction matches students' unique characteristics, students learn at a high rate. When it does not, however, it does not promote nearly the achievement gains that students are capable of. This is the number one reason I do not promote any type of "canned" or pre-programmed reading program. Simply, designers of these programs cannot predict what activities, reading selections, or expectations will work with any particular student.

To teach reading, you have to design instructional opportunities that work for specific students, not the perfectly average child. The instruction has to meet students where they are.

This has implications for how we teach reading. With our reading programs, I have always espoused five principles:

1. Students can only learn the next step;
2. Students need a reason to learn;
3. Assessment and instruction are inseparable;

4. Learning together is better than learning alone; and

5. The instructional approach is more important than the instructional program.

Students can only learn the next step.

This idea is not my own, although I am absolutely convinced it is true. Vygotsky, a researcher in cognitive development, proposed something called the "zone of proximal development." Based on the idea that people learn new ideas and concepts by using what they already know, the zone of proximal development is the point at which one new thing is introduced and all the prior knowledge and ability is used to learn it.

Think about how this applies to reading. A student's abilities and knowledge help the student learn the next concept or skill in reading. The next skill is in the zone of proximal development. In contrast, unless a student has the necessary background, the student cannot learn the skills we try to teach. Those skills are past the zone of proximal development.

It is a mistake to teach students "grade-level skills" when they do not have the background skills, knowledge, and ability to understand them. For example, think about a fourth-grade student who is behind in reading ability. It is a fourth-grade student, so shouldn't you try to teach fourth grade reading skills? Not necessarily. Instead, find out what a student can do and then teach the next step. With this approach, the student will eventually get to fourth-grade ability. Without this approach, it is possible the student never will.

We can teach students day in and day out, and assess the students regularly, but if we do not help them fill in the missing skills, they will get farther and farther behind their grade-level expectations. It is not their fault. No matter how much they try to learn, they simply do not have the ability to grasp the new skills we think they should learn. A better approach is to assess the students first, find out what they can do, and then help them reach the next level. And then the next and the next and the next.

This is the approach we used in our reading programs. We were not concerned with their ability to perform grade-level skills. Instead, we were concerned with their progress toward grade-level expectations, which is fundamentally different. Our students were, on average, pretty far behind their grade-level expectations, around 0.5 to 0.7 grade levels behind in first grade and around 4 grade levels behind in the eighth grade. That is a really big gap to overcome. Only 2% to 3% were on grade level at the pretest. By the end of the semester, on average, around 35% were on grade level.

Students made great progress towards the grade-level expectations because we focused on helping them learn the next step, not on trying to force grade-level skills into brains that were not ready for them. Had we only focused on grade-level skills, we would have set the students, and ourselves, up for failure.

For classroom teachers: This principle will be harder for you to implement than it will be for reading specialists and homeschool teachers. You have a curriculum to follow, and you may be required to teach the skills students are supposed to learn at your grade. You might even have to document the content standards you are teaching. So what are you going to do if the zone of proximal development is not in the curriculum or grade-level standards? This is the time for some rather serious conversations with your supervisors. You have to ask, how important is student learning? Will you be evaluated based on student learning or on adherence to inaccessible expectations? If learning is the goal, then teach students the next step.

For reading interventionists: This principle will be easier for you to implement than for classroom and homeschool teachers. Assess the students when you first start working with them and figure out their next steps. In most schools, the expectations for your instruction are not the same as for teachers. For students you work with, the expectation is progress.

For homeschool teachers: You have a mixed situation. You have a lot of liberty to determine what (and how) students will learn, but you also have to more-or-less address the content standards. On the other hand, you may have a better sense of what your students know and can do. The question for you, therefore, is determining what those next steps should be.

One way that we identified the next steps was to use a rubric that describes not only what students should be able to do at their grade level but also provided the continuum of skills that lead up to the grade-level expectation. Teachers used the rubric to help identify what students could already do, and then looked at the next level for clues about what the students needed to learn next. These rubrics are a decent assessment tool and a great planning tool, which is their purpose.

You can get a copy of the rubrics and a sample tracking form at http://riroadmap.com/grade-level-reading-rubrics.

Students need a reason to learn to read.

Learning to read is a challenge. For some students, it is a bigger challenge, regardless of the reason. It is hard work. Why should students work so hard at this skill? The number one reason anyone learns a new skill is because he or she is interested in the topic, the outcome, or the content. They work hard because they are interested in what they are learning. The learning has a purpose. We can use this concept to teach reading.

Is a student interested in baseball? Use texts about baseball. Is a student interested in horses? Use texts about horses. Etc. (You are reading this book because you are interested in teaching reading.) You get the point.

The actual content of the text, whether fiction or non-fiction, is not important. The important thing is for students to have a reason to read it. They will do the hard work if they want to know more about the topic or are interested in the content. We can use nearly any type of text to teach the skills necessary for reading. Later in this book, we will look at the six skills of reading. Those skills apply to any type of text, so you can use any texts that engage the students' interests.

Yes, there is a time to read about subjects that are, to be honest, not very interesting. We do it to learn about various important topics. However, when we are teaching reading, as opposed to teaching history, math, science, or any other subject, there is no reason not to use texts about topics of interest to the student.

Sometimes, teachers select texts about topics they are interested in or books and stories that they enjoy. That is fine at times, but here we are teaching reading and helping students develop their reading skills. Give students a reason to do the hard work by giving them texts that will be interesting to them.

Here is a good idea: take the students to the library and let them select the books or magazines that are interesting to them. Some books will be too simple; some will be too hard. That is not the point. The point is to find out the topics that interest the students.

Once they have selected their books, have them explain to you and their peers why they choose those texts. You can incorporate the selected materials into your instruction, but, more importantly, you can then find other texts on those topics that are more useful for instruction.

Learning and assessment are integrated.

The traditional model for assessment is to present information and have students do some type of learning activity; give the students an assessment, whether a test, quiz, or demonstration task; and score the assessment to determine how well students learned the information. At this point, one of several things happens.

1. The teacher might score the assessment, give a grade, and let the students know what grade they received.

2. The teacher might review the assessment with the students to provide the correct answers, with or without explaining why some answers are right and others are wrong.

3. The teacher might make corrections, provide some additional instruction, and give the students a chance to try again.

Of the three options, the third option gives students the best chance to learn from their mistakes and improve their skills. But there is a different approach altogether.

In reading instruction, it is possible to integrate assessment into the learning activities. Most of the learning activities based on effective strategies are self-correcting and, therefore, self-assessing. You do not need to do instructional activities and then do assessment activities: they are one and the same. By the time the learning activity is complete, the students have made and corrected mistakes, identified problem areas and worked to solve them, and recognized and mitigated weaknesses. By the time the activity is complete, you will have a sense of students' progress towards meeting expectations, which is the purpose of assessment.

This concept is particularly important for struggling readers. Struggling readers often view reading and reading assessments as something to be feared because they produce a sense of failure. When we combine instruction and assessment, however, every student is able to succeed. In a well-designed lesson, participation leads to learning the skills and passing the assessment at the same time. This approach leads to a sense of engagement, purpose, and success, leading to improved motivation and self-confidence that too many students lack.

As you reflect on your learning activities, consider the following questions.

1. Will students understand the degree to which they have mastered the skill or knowledge?
2. Will students be able to identify their own gaps, weakness, errors, etc.?
3. Does the activity include the opportunity to fill in missing information, expand knowledge, or increase skill levels?
4. Will the students be able to recognize that their skills have increased, from the beginning to the end of the activity?
5. Is the activity sufficiently challenging to provide meaningful instruction, yet designed so that every student can succeed?

Here are a few sample reading activities to demonstrate what this looks like in practice.

Sample activity	How it is self-assessing
Choral Reading (for fluency, phonics, and comprehension)	Students choral read a text multiple times within their small groups until they are able to read the text aloud accurately, and with appropriate pacing and expression.
"Head Words" (for vocabulary and oral language development)	One student places a vocabulary card on his head (so he can't see it), and a partner tries to explain the word well enough for the first student to guess the word. The partner keeps explaining and describing the word/concept until the first student guesses correctly.
Discussion (for comprehension and oral language development)	The teacher keeps asking probing questions until students can express a defensible interpretation of the text.

I-Spy (for phonemic awareness and vocabulary)	Students continue to hunt for (or guess) the object with the correct sound until they find it. Right and wrong guesses are both sounded out and studied.

Later chapters on the six components of reading will provide many strategies and sample activities to help you implement this principle of reading instruction. The sample lesson plans, too, will demonstrate what this looks like in practice.

One advantage to integrating instruction and assessment is that you will not need to put anything in your grade book. By the time the activity is complete, the students will have met the expected level of mastery for the activity.

One of our reading tutors relayed an anecdote related to this topic. At the end of a tutoring session, she asked her students what they enjoyed the most about the session. One of the students told her that the best part was the guided oral reading because he was allowed to keep trying until he got it right! If the tutor were to assign grades for the activity, every student would receive a 100%.

Working together is better than working alone.

Reading is something that we do by ourselves, but learning to read is something that we do together. The best instructional strategies are cooperative in nature, which is why reading instruction uses groups of three or four students. By "cooperative," I mean contributing to each other's learning by playing a meaningful part of the learning process. A cooperative learning activity has the following characteristics.

- Each student in a group has a meaningful role towards a group product or outcome.

- Each student in a group is responsible for helping other students learn.

- Each student in a group is responsible for demonstrating his or her own learning.

When interacting with text, readers draw from their experiences, prior knowledge, skills, memories, and perspectives, and yet students have different experiences, different knowledge, different skills, different memories, and different perspectives. Within a cooperative learning group, each student brings his or her unique characteristics to help other students make sense of—and expand their understanding of—the text.

Some learning activities must be conducted in small groups. For example, you cannot have a discussion by yourself. You cannot perform choral reading by yourself. You cannot understand how people react to word choices if you do not explore how other people interpret words.

On the other hand, some learning activities can be conducted alone. For example, you can have individual students complete a graphic organizer or research more information about a topic. You might ask individual students to group words by a particular sound or a category, such as synonyms. However, the risk of failure is much higher than if the students worked together on these tasks. They risk wasting their time when they could be learning from, and with, each other.

There is a time for individual learning activities. Students can engage in individual activities to prepare them for meaningful participation in cooperative activities. The best learning will come from the cooperative activities. As such, to help students get the most from reading instruction, any individual activities must be followed by cooperative activities. Those cooperative activities will use the individual students' results or products.

For example, individual students may work on a graphic organizer to begin analyzing a text. They can then work with a partner to create one combined graphic organizer. The two students will seek common ideas, as well as new information and ideas. They will discuss each other's ideas to determine what they should or should not include in their joint graphic organizer. Follow-up discussion will give individual students the opportunity to defend and explain their shared ideas, as well as their differing ideas.

One of my core operating principles is "The work we do together is better than the work we do alone." This is equally true for learning. Students have a better chance to learn the content, skills, and concepts when they work cooperatively. They can develop a deeper, more comprehensive understanding of text and overall stronger skills in the reading components. And they will be more engaged in the process of learning and more willing to do the work of learning to read.

We learn together so we can perform alone.

The approach is more important than the program.

When we first proposed working with students in a school or district, many school administrators asked us the same question: "What reading program do you use?" We answered, "None. We follow an approach to instruction rather than a specific program." Many of our tutors asked us, "Where is the curriculum?" The answer to this question was "There isn't one. We have an approach to follow, but not a curriculum." The tutors wanted lesson plans, resources, and schedules. Even if we had a curriculum, it still would not give tutors a plan for what to do and when, or guidance on what would be appropriate for an individual student.

A curriculum has several components, including instructional content, resources, activities, expected outcomes, a sequence for teaching content, and assessment methods. I have seen a lot of curricula over the years, and some of them were really well developed. I also realized that any curriculum is worthless unless it matches what a student needs to learn next, how a student learns, resources that provide learning opportunities, and activities that are engaging to the individual students. Even the best developed curriculum will not guarantee learning if it does not meet a student's needs.

Does this mean you should abandon your curriculum? No. But do consider whether or not it provides appropriate learning opportunities and expectations for the students. We never used a reading program. Instead, we used an "approach," a series of principles for effective instruction. The approach looks like this:

- set up small learning groups,
- develop positive relationships,
- identify and use students' interests to select learning resources,
- assess students' abilities,
- identify next steps for learning,
- address the six reading components every week,
- integrate multiple reading components into single lessons, and
- use learning activities that engage students' interests and address the next step learning.

This approach is how we helped students make huge reading gains. You may find activities or resources from a reading program that will help you follow this approach. Even so, use your judgment about whether the program or curriculum does, in fact, help you follow this approach to meeting students' needs. Most likely, you will need to modify or add to any reading program. Focus on the approach, and use the curriculum or program to help you implement it.

Chapter 3
Defining the Six Components of Reading

Now that we have looked at creating the conditions for learning and the principles for instruction, we turn our attention to WHAT we teach: the six components of reading.

This chapter will provide a brief description of each reading component. In subsequent chapters, we will explore each of them more thoroughly. You can think of this chapter as a quick-and-dirty guide to the six components of reading. Later chapters will examine the reading components more closely, including behaviors, sub-skills, effective and ineffective teaching strategies, sample learning activities, and related components.

These six reading components are not sequential. Students do not have to master one skill before learning another skill. For example, the first skill that students typically begin learning is oral language development. Students do not need to "master" oral language before they can move on to other skills. (In fact, oral language may be the most challenging of all the skills, but at its most simple levels, it is the first skill children begin to learn.)

Similarly, we do not teach one skill at a time. Each reading component is best taught when the instructional activities address multiple components. A single lesson may include opportunities to develop all the skills! In the next chapters, I will discuss which other components to address when focusing on a particular skill.

Now, without delay, here are the six reading components.

Oral Language Development

Definition: Understanding how language is used in a particular event, setting, context, or culture.

Language use varies according to where you are. Concepts and things have different names. Speech may have different patterns, expressions, and phrasing. Language that is appropriate for one situation may not be appropriate for another situation. Understanding these differences is the realm of oral language development. We can apply this understanding to interpreting text by studying how an author (or characters in a story) uses language. Whenever we ask students to analyze how language is used, we are addressing oral language development.

Phonemic Awareness

> *Definition:* The ability to identify and manipulate sounds in words.

Words are made up of sounds. Learning to identify those sounds, change them, remove them, or add to them is phonemic awareness. Close your eyes and think of all the sounds in the word "remote." How many sounds did you hear? (I hear 5 sounds.) Now take out the "re" sound. What word did you just make? That's phonemic awareness. This skill gets progressively more complex, such as when we start talking about syllables or rhythm, which means instruction in phonemic awareness is as valuable for older students as for younger students. Remember: the focus is only on the sounds . . . not reading printed text.

Phonics

> *Definition:* The ability to translate printed symbols into speech sounds.

Another term for phonics is "decoding." At its core, phonics is sounding out written words. This includes how to combine letters into groups to make sounds. Students generally understand more spoken words than printed words. Phonics helps them turn those written words into spoken words. If they then recognize the word, they have a better chance to understand written text. However, simply being able to sound out words is not sufficient for reading. They may be able to sound out the words correctly but still not know what they mean. Reading instruction should help students develop phonics (because phonics are necessary), but only as a part of a broader approach to reading.

Fluency

> *Definition:* The ability to read aloud accurately with appropriate pacing and expression.

Fluency combines several reading skills into one behavior: phonics, comprehension, and oral language. Some reading programs focus only on the accurate reading aloud of words—because that is the only part they can test. This is not fluency but phonics. Fluency is much more than looking at a flash card and correctly naming the word. It is much more than reading a passage aloud and saying most of the words correctly. Real fluency has two more parts that are often overlooked. Is the student reading at an appropriate pace? Does the student use vocal expressions that are appropriate for the text?

Vocabulary

Definition: Knowing the meanings of words and the ability to learn the meanings of new words.

To understand text, you have to know what the words mean. With vocabulary instruction, we help students expand the number of words they know. Students need many more words than we can teach them, so we also teach them a process for figuring out the meanings of new words.

Comprehension

Definition: Developing a justifiable, personal interpretation of a text.

Comprehension is much more than knowing what the words mean in a text, or content knowledge. It also includes the ability to analyze, synthesize, and evaluate a text. These skills apply to both fiction and non-fiction texts. Students apply their background knowledge, experiences, and perspectives to the analysis process to create their own interpretations of texts, and they are able to justify or explain how they arrived at that interpretation.

Chapter 4
Oral Language Development

Oral Language Development is the most sophisticated of all the reading skills. It is the first skill that children begin learning, and it is the one skill that people continue learning throughout life—whether or not they know it!

Definition

> The ability to understand how language is used in a particular event, setting, context, or culture.

Before we go any further, I will take a moment to define the terms in the definition. (This will help you develop your own oral language skills because you will have a better idea of what these words mean in the context of this book!)

Understand:	Ability to make sense or develop an interpretation
Language:	Individual words and words in a string that are intended to express an idea
Event:	An occurrence or events in a single time and place
Setting:	A type of location or place
Context:	Conditions, framework, or social environment in which language use occurs
Culture:	The expectations, rules, experiences, and beliefs shared by two or more people

"Oral Language Development" is better described as "Oral Language Skills." Oral language development simply refers to the process of developing one's oral language skills. Typically, when people describe oral language skills, they are talking about very young children learning how express themselves, such as by naming things, speaking in complete sentences, or understanding and answering simple questions. However, oral language skills go far, far beyond these basic skills.

If we think about what is happening with oral language development, we see that what we are really teaching children is how to communicate in various events, settings, contexts, and cultures. For example:

- When we instruct children to use their "inside voice," we are really telling them that in the "inside" setting, there are different rules for talking than there are for the "outside" setting.

- When we tell children to say "please" and "thank you," we are instructing them on the rules for communicating based on the expectations of our culture.

- When we teach children that the way we talk at home or with friends may not be the same as how we talk to people in authority, we let them know that there are different rules for different contexts.

All of this is oral language development.

Oral Language and Young Children

At the lowest level of oral language skills, children learn to name objects and use basic speech patterns. For example, a parent might pick up a ball and say, "Ball. Do you want the ball?" The parent is telling the child that the object he or she is holding is called a ball, that "ball" is the word in the parents' language for the object. The child learns that to indicate the object to the parent, the child needs to use the word "ball."

If a parent asks the child, "Do you want to go outside?" the parent is modeling how the child can put words together to ask a question. The parent is demonstrating what he or she thinks is the acceptable way to put the words together. If the parent asks, instead, "Go outside?" the parent teaches the child that that is an acceptable way, too.

Basic speech patterns and vocabulary are not the entirety of oral language skills. These behaviors represent only a small part of oral language, only a few of the many and complex oral language skills.

Some people may consider that oral language instruction is only for very young children. For example, in many school environments, teaching and reinforcing oral language generally focuses on children under five or six years old. The focus on very young children's oral language skills is extremely important.

Oral language builds the foundation for the ability to communicate: both to understand received information and to express information.

I have known children who have very poor oral language skills. Even at the age of three or four years old, they are still pointing at objects they want and making meaningless sounds. They do not have the words to name objects or express their desires. Other children may still talk in "baby talk" when they are in kindergarten or first grade. They may be unable to understand simple questions and provide a meaningful response. With so few words at their disposal and with little to no grasps of the syntax of language, these children are going to have a really tough time learning to read.

I understand why early childhood educators focus on oral language development and why many people think oral language development is for young children. I understand the value of helping students develop basic speech patterns and vocabulary. Instruction in basic and low-level oral language skills is important when working with very young children. Unfortunately, once children have more or less accomplished those low-level skills, explicit instruction stops.

Based on the thousands of teachers I have worked with through our reading tutoring program and prior similar programs, I know that few teachers past about third or fourth grade ever think about oral language skills, much less provide any explicit instruction in oral language skills. This is a problem. As communication situations and ideas become more complex, as expectations for comprehension and expression increase, and as children encounter a wider variety of cultures, they need increasingly stronger and more sophisticated oral language skills.

Breaking Down Oral Language Skills

Oral Language is not a single skill but a collection of five sub-skills:

> *Vocabulary:* learning and using the names of things, ideas and concepts, processes, etc.; learning to differentiate between idiomatic, local definitions and universally accepted definitions; learning to identify, use, and interpret connotative meanings of words and phrases

> *Syntax:* learning and using grammatically correct sentence structure; learning and using the rules of language usage

Morphological Skills: understanding word parts, roots, affixes, etc.; understanding how interactions among words affect their meaning

Pragmatics: learning to use language effectively to accomplish a purpose; learning how to modify language as appropriate for the context, setting, and culture

Phonological Skills: learning to identify and modify sounds within words

Instruction in any of these sub-skills contributes to a student's oral language development. If you provide instruction in each area, you will help students develop strong oral language skills that will help them communicate not only when speaking and listening but also when writing and reading.

Explaining These Sub-skills

Early Oral Language Learning

Two of these sub-skills can be developed fairly early in life: phonological skills and syntax.

Phonological skills: Most people learn phonological skills at a young age, perhaps before age six or seven. Children who do not develop phonological skills are at great risk of reading difficulties later. Many of the students whom we tutored struggled with phonological skills. They needed explicit instruction and practice in identifying and manipulating sounds within words. Because the connection between phonological skills and reading ability is so strong, we insisted that tutors provide instruction in phonological skills at all grade levels. The results show that this approach was successful. I will discuss this topic more thoroughly in the chapter on phonemic awareness.

Syntax: Students learn syntax by the end of fourth or fifth grade, right? Not so in many cases. Even the most cursory examination of students' writing reveals that many students have a weak grasp of syntax. Many adults, too, admit to difficulty with grammar. This is a big deal. Changes to the grammatical structure of a sentence can change its meaning. For example, the sentences "I have been to the movies" and "I went to the movies" mean different things. Without a good understanding of syntax, we may have difficulty communicating our ideas clearly, and we may have difficulty interpreting what other people say and write.

Life-long Oral Language Learning

The other three oral language sub-skills continue to develop throughout a person's life: vocabulary, morphological skills, and pragmatics.

Vocabulary: We learn new words, new meanings, and new connotations as we read more and have more interactions with different types of people. We do not simply learn definitions of words. Instead, we develop our understanding of how words are used, how similar words can express various ideas, how people use different words to express the same idea, and how people interpret word usage.

For example, think about the words "orient" and "oriental." These words mean "east" and "eastern," respectively. Once upon a time, people from China, Japan, and other nearby countries were called "Orientals." This is no longer appropriate. Now we say "Asian." The terminology has changed because the interpretation of, and response to, the term "oriental" has changed. Within the context of oral language skills, learning how words are used and interpreted is the sub-skill of vocabulary.

Morphological skills: In connection with vocabulary, we develop our morphological skills to expand our understanding of how words can be modified to express different ideas. Also, we learn how to interpret changes in word order and how changes in sentence structure can affect interpretation.

For example, consider the sentences "Absolutely, this is the truth" and "This is the absolute truth." The first sentence implies an agreement about the truth. In contrast, the second sentence implies that the "truth" is entirely correct and not subject to debate. By changing the word order, the speaker or writer has changed how the sentences are interpreted. Morphological skills help students understand these differences in interpretation.

Pragmatics: We use language to accomplish a purpose. What we say, how we say it, and whom we say it to affects whether or not we accomplish that purpose. As our pragmatics skills develop and improve, we learn the expectations for communicating in various contexts, settings, and cultures so that we can accomplish our purposes.

For example, our skill with pragmatics may determine whether we say "Give me a raise," "I want a raise," or "I believe I deserve a raise." Each of these three statements communicates the same basic idea, but they may provoke very different reactions. When we use our pragmatics skills, we think about what our purpose is, who the listener or reader is, and how we might best communicate our ideas.

Most importantly, perhaps, we become better at understanding what other people mean when they speak or write, and we learn how to communicate appropriately so that we can build positive relationships with others.

This is the reason why I say that oral language skills are the most sophisticated of all the reading skills: the learning never stops.

Connection to Reading

The National Reading Panel had very little to say about oral language, mainly because it is oral. But if we think about how we use oral language skills, what those skills are for, we see that they transfer directly to making meaning from text, i.e., reading. Oral language skills focus on learning how language is used to communicate ideas, which includes in text.

Think about something you recently read and then consider the following questions.

- What writing style did the author use?
- Was the writing casual or formal?
- What types of words did the author use?
- What implications did the author convey, beyond the actual words?
- How did the author use sentence structure, grammar, and punctuation to communicate clearly (or not)?
- Did the author write the way you would write?

(If you read a story with characters, you could ask these same questions about the way the characters speak. Not only will this contribute to oral language development but also it will contribute to increased comprehension.)

Did you try to answer the questions? If so, then you were analyzing text by using oral language skills. You applied your oral language skills to reading. We help students learn to do this, as well. As it turns out, not only do students strengthen their comprehension of the text but also they form impressions of the author's credibility, character, and competence.

We use these skills when listening, and we can use them when reading. Whenever we help students analyze the way language is used in text, we are helping them develop and then use oral language skills.

What Works for Oral Language Instruction

Now that you have an understanding of the sub-skills for oral language, you have many clues for the types of strategies and activities to help students develop oral language. In brief, any activities that engage students in those sub-skills will contribute to oral language. If you use those activities with text, you help students develop their reading comprehension.

Here is the caveat: You need to use strategies for ALL the sub-skills.

In my observation of teachers and in my review of instructional plans for thousands of reading tutors, however, I noted that teachers for younger students tend to focus only on basic (non-nuanced) vocabulary and phonological skills. As students advance to upper elementary, teachers tend to focus on connotative/nuanced vocabulary and syntax. Not until students get to middle or high school do teachers begin to focus on morphological skills and pragmatics. In part, I believe, they do this because simple vocabulary and phonological skills are least complex to grasp and morphological skills and pragmatics are most complex. This is a mistake.

Students at all ages can learn—or begin learning—all the oral language sub-skills. The more complex skills, such as pragmatics, and the more complex concepts, such context-dependent expectations, might be presented in simple forms for younger children, but children can learn them if the teacher uses effective and appropriate strategies.

Although you can use many different activities to teach oral language skills, effective activities can be grouped within five types of strategies.

Five Strategies for Teaching Oral Language Skills

- Modeling
- Analysis
- Practice with correction and reflection

- Discussion

- Explicit instruction

Truly, all five strategies are necessary to help students develop their oral language skills, which means you need to design activities that employ all five strategies. Although it is possible to address all the strategies through one carefully designed, comprehensive activity, you might need several activities. The only strategy that you will use all the time is modeling.

Modeling: Your primary responsibility as a reading teacher is to conscientiously and consistently model the language use that is appropriate for an event, setting, context, or culture. Children learn to speak according to what they hear, so your job is to make sure they hear appropriate language use. Exposure to language leads to familiarity, which, in turn, leads to students' ability to use language in that same manner.

Under the modeling strategy, you are using language in a certain manner and helping students understand what you are doing and why. How do you want students to communicate? What types of language usage or patterns do you want them to learn? If you don't model it, they won't learn it. Modeling is not restricted to specific times, activities, or content areas. It is what you do all the time, every time, and in every place. If students can hear you speak, you are modeling language use.

Normally, you are communicating with students in an academic context, within the culture of learning that you create in your classroom. This means you need to use academic language: precise and concise explanations, grammatically correct sentences, and standard vocabulary that avoids colloquial or idiomatic expressions. As you engage students individually or in non-classroom settings, you might modify your language use. In either case, you need to explicitly describe the language expectations, model their use, and prompt students to adhere to those expectations.

Analysis: Analysis means developing conclusions about language use. To help students develop oral language skills, you teach them to perform three types of analysis: (a) Word Analysis, which is analyzing word parts and their effect on meaning; (b) Text Analysis, which is analyzing the way the author or characters use language; and (c) Message Analysis, which is analyzing the author's intention, purpose, and content.

To a certain degree, analysis strategies use text to provide modeling, and activities engage students in analyzing how language is used in the text. Activities provide students with opportunities to do one or more types of analysis. As you design or reflect on your instructional activities, make sure that students have the opportunity to do all three types.

Practice with correction and reflection: Oral language is a set of skills. Like other skills, such as playing an instrument or learning a craft, development takes guidance, opportunities for practice, and reflection on results supported by correction. Which is followed by more guidance, more practice, and more reflection supported by correction.

Students need many opportunities to communicate (whether in speech or writing), and you, the teacher, need to provide correction and help students think about how they are using language in a specific event, setting, context, or culture. As with modeling, you do this all the time. However, you can also design specific activities to provide practice with feedback.

You need to make a judgment call when providing feedback. On the one hand, if students understand the difference between appropriate and inappropriate language (as determined by the event, setting, context, or culture) but choose to use inappropriate language, the correction may be punitive. More commonly, if students have not yet learned that difference—or have not learned the reason for the difference—the correction needs to be instructional with the opportunity to try again. Language takes a lifetime of practice.

Discussion: Discussion brings all the strategies together. The teacher provides questions for student response and facilitates students asking and responding to questions from each other. Questions address various levels from Bloom's Taxonomy, Depth of Knowledge, or similar systems of interacting with text.

Explicit instruction: Language follows a series of patterns: patterns for word use, patterns of sentence structure, patterns for volume and tone, etc. With explicit instruction, you teach students the patterns that are appropriate for various settings, events, contexts, and cultures. You teach them, "In this place, for this purpose, here is how you say...."

I will address discussion and explicit instruction more fully next.

The Number One Strategy: Discussion

Remember, the definition of oral language development is learning how language is used in a particular event, setting, context, or culture. People do this by experiencing a wide variety of language uses, analyzing how people communicate, identifying patterns, relating language usage to results, and testing assumptions about communicating.

The number one strategy for helping students develop their oral language skills is discussion. Discussion is not about responding to questions with the "right" answer. Discussion is

- sharing one's own ideas,
- asking questions,
- agreeing and disagreeing,
- explaining and defending a position,
- contributing more information, and
- expanding on others' ideas.

In the context of reading, we discuss language use, whether the author's or the characters'. Your job, as the teacher, is to ask open-ended questions that provoke and permit discussion about the language. For example, if two characters, Bob and Tom, are having a disagreement, you could ask the following questions for discussion.

1. Do Bob and Tom seem to be agreeing or disagreeing? What are they disagreeing about? (Setting the stage for the discussion of language use)

2. How do you know that they are disagreeing? What did Bob say that makes you think he disagrees with Tom?

3. Are they talking nicely or meanly (e.g., is the disagreement respectful, hostile, friendly, derogatory, angry, sarcastic)? What makes you think that?

4. What is another way they could talk to each other and what other words might they use?

5. Thinking about the actual words used, how did Tom react when Bob disagreed? Was that the reaction Bob wanted? If not, how else might Bob have expressed his disagreement?

6. What would be the difference between saying "You're wrong," "I think you're wrong," "I don't agree," "Bob, that is not true," and "That's stupid"? How might these different ways get different reactions from Tom? How does the message change with these different ways?

7. Tom could say "You ARE wrong" or "YOU are wrong"? How does the emphasis change the meaning?

8. If their relationship were different, such as a boss and an employee or as two friends, how might they talk differently?

9. What are some ways you expressed disagreement and what kind of response did you get? How might you have expressed disagreement differently?

As you can see, discussion goes far beyond simple recall. Instead, the questions need to reflect all the levels of Bloom's Taxonomy, Depth of Knowledge, or similar systems for categorizing interactions with text. If you limit the questions to the simplest levels or superficial who, what, when, and where types of questions, you are not helping students understand or analyze the text; you are only testing their recall. There will be no reason for discussion.

I will address question types more thoroughly in the chapter on comprehension. Regarding oral language skills, the central theme of the discussion questions is how the author or characters are using, or could use, language. Overall, we use discussion to help students be aware of the interaction among language, message, and purpose.

Integrating Oral Language Development and Comprehension through Discussion

One great advantage to using discussion is that it integrates easily with the number one strategy for developing comprehension, which is also discussion! With the right discussion questions, you can address oral language and comprehension at the same time. In fact, you can not fully address comprehension without addressing oral language: understanding language use leads to understanding the text.

The Number Two Strategy: Explicit Instruction

You can explicitly teach students language patterns to use, and you can tell them how those patterns are interpreted. Examples include the following.

- Remember to say "Please."
- Call him "Mr. Wilson," not "bro."
- Saying "I ain't got no" is incorrect. Say "I don't have" instead.
- If you call people "stupid," they won't like you.
- When you get to the bank, tell the clerk, "I would like to open an account. Is there someone who can assist me?"
- Don't be offended if they call you "son." That's just how they talk here.
- Make sure to use correct grammar and avoid contractions.

When you provide explicit instruction in language use, you provide the patterns to use in various events, settings, contexts, and cultures. For many students, especially those with limited exposure to language use outside of a familiar context (family, friends, local community), explicit instruction can be useful.

Using Explicit Instruction to Enhance Reading Comprehension

Once students have a grasp of the language "rules" for a particular event, setting, context, or culture, you can ask students to analyze text to see the degree to which those rules have been applied by the author or characters. Students can use their understanding of language usage to analyze and evaluate the content, such as the author's credibility or a character's personality or background.

For example, you can have the students write a response to a prompt, such as

- "Does the author use correct grammar? How does that affect your confidence in the author's knowledge of the topic?"; or
- "Did the character speak appropriately to his uncle?"

After students write their responses, they should share their responses and discuss each others' responses to hear various interpretations and strengthen or modify their own understanding.

Which, of course, brings us right back to discussion. Engaging students in discussion after they write a reflection is a good strategy for helping students strengthen their oral language skills. The writing exercise helps them reflect on the text and their own understanding, and it prepares them to participate meaningfully in discussion.

The one thing you absolutely do not want to do is collect their responses, grade them, and move on to the next topic. If their responses are not particularly complete or if their ideas are not defensible, students need the opportunity to develop a better analysis and interpretation. Otherwise, they will have learned nothing other than the fact that they got it wrong. On the other hand, if you provide feedback or engage students in follow-up discussion, they have the opportunity to expand their understanding and improve their own skills.

Sample Activities for Oral Language Development

Strategy	Sample Activities Types	Oral Language Sub-skills
Modeling	Continuous demonstration by the teacher or other adults	Vocabulary
		Syntax
		Morphological Skills
		Pragmatics
Analysis	Creating word groups and modifying words	All sub-skills
	Rhyming and "word play"	
	Close reading	
	Writing to prompts	
	Discussion	
	Character analysis	
	Direct instruction	
	Cause and effect study	

Practice with Reflection and Correction	Teaching language patterns	Vocabulary
		Syntax
	Guided oral reading / choral reading	Morphological Skills
	Reading and writing skits or plays	Pragmatics
	Revising and rewording	
	Writing to prompts	
	Short-answer questions	
	Direct instruction	
Discussion	Writing to prompts followed by student discussion	All sub-skills
	Graphic organizers followed by student discussion	
	Student-created questions followed by student discussion	
	Text analysis followed by student discussion	
Explicit instruction	Teaching language patterns	All sub-skills
	Revising and rewording	
	Direct instruction	
	Discussion	
	Character analysis	

What Does Not Work for Oral Language Instruction

If you are guided by the instructional strategies for oral language development, as well as the sub-skills that students need to learn, you can find or design many effective instructional activities. On the other hand, four common instructional strategies are either not effective or minimally effective.

Strategy	Reason Why It Does Not Work
Sustained Silent Reading (SSR)	SSR does not require analysis, practice, correction, reflection, or discussion. There is no opportunity to interpret language use from multiple perspectives. SSR might help strengthen existing skills, but it does not help expand or increase skills.
Worksheets	Worksheets cannot engage students in analysis, discussion, practice, or reflection. There is no exploration of ideas or opportunities to interpret text/language from multiple perspectives. You could use some types of worksheets, such as graphic organizers, to help students prepare for discussion. By themselves, however, they are not effective for developing oral language skills.
Individual Work (other than worksheets)	When students work individually, they do not have the opportunity to reflect on or discuss text from multiple perspectives and can not broaden their understanding of language use. You could use some types of individual work as a preliminary step to help students prepare their ideas for discussion.

Computerized Instruction	Computerized instructional programs may assist somewhat with phonological skills or vocabulary, but they cannot assist with pragmatics and morphological skills. Those skills are too complex and too dependent upon individual interpretation, situational analysis, context, and culture. Computerized instruction is also very poor for helping students understand syntax.

Companion Reading Components

Oral language skills are best taught when combined with instruction in the following four reading components. As you are helping students develop their oral language skills, also provide instruction in these components.

Phonemic Awareness: The oral language phonological sub-skill overlaps with the skills students learn during phonemic awareness instruction. As such, you can help students improve their phonological skills while improving their phonemic awareness, and vice-versa.

Vocabulary: The reading component of vocabulary comprises learning the meaning of words, the interpretation of words, and the process for learning new words. The vocabulary reading component contributes to oral language skills by expanding students' word knowledge, while the oral language skills assist with interpretation of the words. Together, they lead to increased overall comprehension.

Fluency: The emphasis on accurate decoding in fluency contributes to students' phonological and morphological sub-skills. Furthermore, the fluency emphasis on pacing and expression contribute to a better understanding of how an author or character is using language to convey information. When we teach students to vary their pacing and expression for fluency, we are also helping students understand how to modify language use or oral language skills.

Comprehension: As students improve their comprehension skills, they learn to create a defensible interpretation of the text. Part of this process is understanding how the author or characters use language, gauging the effectiveness of language use for a purpose, and analyzing the appropriateness of the language. The skills students develop in comprehension and the skills they learn in oral language development depend on each other: they cannot be used and, therefore, cannot be taught in isolation.

Chapter 5
Phonemic Awareness

Phonemic awareness is a strong predictor of a child's ability to read well. Children with strong phonemic awareness skills are more likely to read on grade level than children without this necessary skill. Phonemic awareness is, in great part, a necessary precursor to phonics, print vocabulary, fluency, and comprehension. So what is it, exactly?

Definition

> The ability to identify sounds within spoken words and to manipulate those sounds to make other words.

For example, you are using phonemic awareness skills if you can

- say the individual sounds in "carbonate"
- identify the difference between "carbonate" and "carbonation"
- pick out the similar sounds in "carbonate" and "incarcerate"
- find the two stressed syllables in "carbonate"
- replace the "ate" sound in "carbonate" with "ize"

Later, I will discuss the various sub-skills in phonemic awareness, as well as instructional strategies. In the meantime, if you can perform these simple tasks, you are demonstrating phonemic awareness.

Phonemic awareness is not phonics. With phonics, you convert text into speech, but with phonemic awareness, you only focus on the sounds.

> Phonics = sounding out written words.

> Phonemic awareness = identifying and manipulating spoken sounds.

They are closely linked, but they are not the same.

Although it may seem obvious to us as adults, the idea that words are not single units but collections of sounds requires a cognitive leap for most children. After all, we speak in complete words, and whole words have specific meanings. Children grasp whole words easily, but then we ask them to pick out the parts within words, which often do not have any meaning of their own. It is an "a ha" moment for children when they realize this concept. All of phonemic awareness stems from that conceptual understanding.

Phonemic Awareness Is for All Students

Instruction in phonemic awareness can begin when children are quite young, certainly before they enter kindergarten. If students miss, or fall behind, in this critical skill, they will struggle to read. They will already be behind in learning the foundational skills that lead to grade-level reading. And they will fall farther and farther behind in reading as they get older. Based on our student data, I believe that much of the later reading difficulties can be explained by students' poor phonemic awareness.

We required our tutors to address phonemic awareness at all grade levels, even with students in middle and high school. Students certainly can have, and should have, strong phonemic awareness skills by that age. However, if students in upper grades are struggling to read, there is a strong possibility that they have poor foundational skills, particularly phonemic awareness.

With our requirement that all teachers provide phonemic awareness instruction, we saw students in middle and high school making two, three, and even four grade-level jumps in their reading ability. We saw many students in elementary school making greater than a grade-level gain during a single semester. Simply put, students need the foundational skills so they can learn the more advanced skills. (See "Students can only learn the next step" in chapter two.)

Common Misconceptions Regarding Phonemic Awareness

1. Children will grasp phonemic awareness naturally, such as through nursery rhymes and songs.

2. Children past a certain grade, such as first or second grade, will have mastered phonemic awareness and do not require any additional instruction.

3. Phonemic awareness skills, in general, do not progress beyond a first or second grade level, i.e., there is no more to learn.

The first two assumptions are mistakes because, obviously,

students are not mastering phonemic awareness skills. Their reading difficulties indicate that they are not grasping phonemic awareness, and later instruction in phonemic awareness produces measurable reading improvement.

Common reading assessments may indicate that a student has "mastered" phonemic awareness, but assessments may not measure phonemic awareness skills past the second grade or third grade. The assessments we used for our reading programs had this problem. The pre-test results would indicate that students had achieved mastery, leading tutors to believe that they did not need to provide any instruction in this reading skill (in spite of our requirements). We had to teach them what "mastery" meant: "mastery" meant only that the student had achieved second grade level. For a student in second grade, that was fine; for a student in third grade or higher, not so much.

The third assumption is a mistake because, frankly, phonemic awareness skills become more sophisticated than the level taught in the lowest elementary grades. Phonemic awareness progresses from individual sounds to patterns, enunciation, accents, meters, and rhythms. For example, teachers generally introduce the concept of poetic meters around the fourth or fifth grade. The ability to identify meter, with a regular pattern and number of accented and unaccented syllables, is a phonemic awareness skill.

The bottom line: Most students struggling to read will benefit from explicit instruction in phonemic awareness, and all students benefit from instruction in increasingly sophisticated phonemic awareness skills.

Breaking Down Phonemic Awareness Skills

Phonemic Awareness is more than listening for sounds in words. Rather, it is one primary skill that is reinforced and demonstrated through eight sub-skills.

Primary Skill: Identification

Identification is the ability to break words into individual sounds. Example: What three sounds do you hear in the word "cheese"?

If a student can accurately and consistently identify the sounds within words, then he or she can likely do (or learn to do) all the rest of the sub-skills.

Phonemic Awareness Sub-skills

In alphabetical order, the eight sub-skills to phonemic awareness are as follows.

Blending: connecting individual sounds to make a word, the opposite of identification. (example: What word do you get when you combine the sounds "ch," "ee," and "z"?)

Completion: predicting the next sound in a partial word. (example: What sound can follow "chee"?)

Deletion: removing specific sounds from a word. (example: What word do you get if you remove the "ch" sound from "cheese"?)

Differentiation: recognizing that two sounds are different or that sounds in words are different. (example: Are these words the same or different: "cheese" "these"?)

Isolation: identifying specific sounds within words. (example: What is the final sound in the word "cheese"?)

Manipulation: replacing or changing sounds within words. (example: Change the "ch" sound in "cheese" with a "th" sound.)

Matching: finding words that have the same sounds in a specific place in a word. (examples: What word has the same second sound as "cheese"? "What word has the same final sound as "cheese"?)

Reversal: switching the order of two sounds in a word. (example (non-cheese example): What word do you get if you switch the "d" and "f" sounds in "defer"?)

I will add one more skill to this list: Emphatics. Emphatics is recognizing accents in words and stress (emphasis) given to spoken words. For example, a person who says "I don't *want* cheese; I *need* cheese" is emphasizing the difference between want and need. Emphatics is not typically included as a phonemic awareness skill, but it is a phonological skill. (Phonemic awareness is a subset of phonological awareness, an understanding of sound within language.) I include emphatics here because it relates to the ability to analyze sounds within words and passages. It leads to understanding meter, rhythm, and similar auditory characteristics of speech.

Emphatics is also a cross-over skill with oral language development because it relates to changing spoken sounds to communicate a message, i.e., how a speaker emphasizes certain words or sounds. For example, if a person says "I am STILL waiting," he is communicating frustration by emphasizing the word "still.")

Integrated Approach to Phonemic Awareness Skills

Students do not have to master one skill before learning another skill. They are not sequential, other than the focus on the primary skill, which should be introduced first and continue to be reinforced as you help students perform the sub-skills.

For example, the student doesn't need to focus only on identification before tackling matching. In fact, a good lesson in phonemic awareness will combine several sub-skills. Not only will this make the learning activity more interesting but also it will help students think about the sounds in multiple ways, further reinforcing their ability to perform the primary skill: identify sounds within words.

On the other hand, some sub-skills are more challenging than others because they take greater cognitive processing and analysis. Very generally, blending, completion, differentiation, and isolation are less sophisticated than deletion, emphatics, manipulation, matching, and reversal.

If you are working with young children, say around ages three to four, I recommend that you stick to the simplest sub-skills. Once students are pretty good at finding the individual sounds within words and a few of the simpler sub-skills, they will be able to pick up the other sub-skills more easily as their cognitive development progresses. With these young children, you are helping them make that cognitive leap from whole words to sounds within words. If you are working with older children, try presenting activities that address the more challenging sub-skills.

Principles for Phonemic Awareness Instruction

The research is quite clear about principles for phonemic awareness instruction. We will look at instructional strategies next, but all effective strategies and instructional activities are based on the same three principles, as follows.

1. Instruction needs to be explicit and systematic.
2. Instruction should focus on only one or two phonemes at

a time.

3. Instruction follows a "continuum of complexity."

Explicit and Systematic

"Explicit" means the instruction will clearly focus on specific sounds. As you plan instruction in phonemic awareness, complete this sentence: "Students will focus on the [fill in the blank] sound." With explicit instruction, pre-determine which sounds students will use as they learn the various phonemic awareness sub-skills. The opposite of explicit instruction is "implicit" instruction, in which case you hope students will naturally figure out how sounds work in words through a lot of exposure. What the research says: Explicit instruction works well; implicit instruction does not.

"Systematic" means having a plan for what you will do first, second, third, etc. It means knowing what sounds students will study and the order in which they will study them.

For example, with youngest children, you will spend a lot of time on rhyming words. Once students understand what "rhyming" means, you might concentrate on words that end with the "-ack" sound, then move to the "-ish" sound, and then study words with the "-eek" sound. Later, you might move to words with the same starting sounds. You might focus on words that begin with "b", then move to "c" and then to "l".

The point of systematic instruction is to plan ahead what you will teach and when. The opposite of systematic instruction is random instruction, which I call chaotic instruction. Chaotic instruction does not work for phonemic awareness. Systematic instruction is necessary to help students build mental patterns for sounds within words.

Focus on One or Two Phonemes

Even as adults, if you get too much information at once, your ability to understand, retain, and use the information drops off pretty quickly. This consideration is even more pronounced in children. They simply cannot process and build mental patterns on many concepts at once.

Think about learning to touch type on a keyboard. You have all the keys in front of you, so you should be able to type every word correctly on day one, right? Of course not. Instead, you begin learning a few simple patterns, perhaps with common words, and you practice them until you can type them correctly without thinking. Later, you practice a few new patterns. Eventually, you are pretty good with the entire keyboard and you have fairly good accuracy. This works because our brains are exceptional at creating patterns.

A large part of teaching students to read is helping them develop mental patterns and understanding how language works. If they try to focus on too many concepts or too much information at once, they won't develop those patterns. The brain simply cannot do it. Conversely, if they begin to develop mental patterns based on a limited set of information, they will be able to apply that understanding and use those mental patterns to grasp new information later.

This is true with instruction in phonemic awareness. What the research says, and what we told out tutors to follow, is to focus only on one or two phonemes at a time. Once students can consistently find them, use them, change them, etc., then—and only then—do we go on to another set of phonemes. With a concentrated focus on only one or two phonemes, students brains will actually develop the strong neurological connections needed to gain phonemic awareness.

With phonemic awareness instruction, we are not trying to teach everything there is to know and do, at least not all at once. Instead, we are helping students understand how sounds work within words, how they can find them, and how those sounds can be changed.

Bottom line: focus on one or two phonemes until students can consistently demonstrate their understanding of those sounds. Then move on to the next one or two.

Continuum of Complexity

Some sounds are easier to identify than others. Some sub-skills are easier to perform than others. For both sounds and skills, there is a continuum of complexity, from least complex to most complex and from the simplest to the most difficult. Everyone starts at the lowest level of these continua.

Continuum of Complexity: Sound Types

Based on the continuum of skill types (see below), students can perform a variety of actions before they advance to phonemic awareness, including finding rhymes, recognizing different sounding words, and counting syllables within words. Once students begin to understand that words are collections of unique sounds, you can begin to address phonemic awareness skills.

Start with easy sounds first, and then advance to more challenging sounds. Easy sounds are hard and soft consonants, and long and short vowel sounds, particularly those produced by individual letters. Easy sounds are those sounds that do not require you to move your mouth when you make them. These sounds are fairly easy to identify with a little practice.

Farther up the continuum of sound complexity are diphthongs, which are vowel sounds that make the mouth and tongue move when producing them. These are harder to pick up because they are made of several sounds at once. As students develop their phonemic awareness, they learn to pick out the individual parts of sounds. For example, the word "way" has three separate sounds. The "w" sound and the two sounds within the "ay".

Along with diphthongs are blends and digraphs. Blends are created when you combine two consonants but can hear two sounds, such as the "pl" sound. Digraphs are created when you combine two consonants and you can only hear one sound, such as the "th" sound. These are a little more challenging to recognize. Many children who struggle to read have a hard time identifying what sound, or sounds, they are hearing in blends and digraphs.

Eventually, with effective instruction, students advance to the point where they can identify vocalized and non-vocalized sounds (those that make the vocal chords vibrate or not), aspirated and non-aspirated sounds (those followed by a puff of air or not), and the schwa sound (the "uh" sound that unaccented single vowels make).

Your role is to find out what types of sounds the student can consistently identify, and then select the next step in the continuum of complexity for sounds. If you introduce sound types that are too complex, the student will not be able to perform the phonemic awareness skills with those sounds.

My best advice: Assume the student is at the bottom of the continuum and have the student demonstrate sub-skills with easy sounds. Then, quickly move up to more complex sounds until the student begins to make mistakes. That point is where your instruction will begin.

Continuum of Complexity: Skill Types

Children do not have an inborn understanding of sounds within

Teaching Phonemic Awareness

words. As mentioned previously, most students can naturally grasp an understanding of whole words and the concept that words have meaning, but it is quite a leap from whole words to parts of words.

In fact, most students can perform a host of skills before they begin analyzing and manipulating sounds within words. The following skill continuum describes the skills according to the approximate age students can perform them with instruction and practice.

Age Range	Skills
Before age 5	Imitate simple rhymes
	Recognize what words do not rhyme
Within age 5	Recognize when word sounds have been changed
	Count out (such as clap) syllables within words
	Blending initial sounds of words with the remainder of the word (example: l – og)
	Find rhyming words (example: What rhymes with "log"?)
	Identify initial sounds (example: What is the first sound in "log"?)
Within age 6	Remove part of a compound word (example: Say "watermelon" but without "water." What do you get?)
	Remove a syllable (example: Say "melon" but without "mel." What word do you get?)
	Blend 2-, 3-, and 4-phoneme, 1-syllable words, with and without blends (example: What word do you get from c – a – t?)
	Substitute phonemes to make a new 1-syllable words (example: What word do you get if you change the "h" in "hat" to a "k" sound?)

Within age 7	Remove the first or last non-blended sounds of 1-syllable words (example: Say "door" but leave out the "d" sound. What word do you get?)
Within age 8	Remove the first sound of a word that begins with a blended sound (example: What word do you get if you remove the "k" sound from "clean"?)
Within age 9	Remove inner or ending sounds of words with blended sounds (example: Can you say "blend" without the "b" sound? example: If you remove the "s" sound from "dusk," what word do you get?)

(adapted from Moats and Tolman's article "The Development of Phonological Skills")

The most important thing to notice from this continuum is that it is, actually, a continuum. Not only do the skills get more challenging over time but also the later skills are more advanced versions of early skills.

This means that students need to learn the simpler skills to get ready to learn the more difficult skills. Students will only learn the more challenging skills if they have learned the simpler skills first.

As with the continuum of sound types, we cannot assume that students have learned the earlier skills when we first start working with them. Instead, if we are going to find the appropriate next step in learning, we try out those early skills with students, see if they can do them consistently, and then move up the continuum until the student starts to struggle. In this way, we find out what students already know and what they are able to learn next.

One last thing about this continuum of skill complexity: it does not end at age 9, as suggested in the chart. This chapter has provided many examples of higher, more challenging skills.

What Works for Phonemic Awareness Instruction

As long as you follow the principles of phonemic awareness instruction, you can devise and implement many different strategies that will help students develop their phonemic awareness skills. In fact, you will want to use many different strategies. When you use multiple strategies while focusing on the same phonemes or sub-skills, your students will develop strong skills that they can eventually use easily and naturally.

The following list of strategies is a partial list. These are a few strategies that we know will work, but you may find or use others. The only caveat is this: any strategies you use must follow the instructional principles described previously.

Six Sample Strategies for Teaching Phonemic Awareness

- Modeling
- Question and answer / Oral response
- Sound searching and identification
- Rhyming poetry and songs
- Repetition and restructuring
- Phoneme / Sound counting

Modeling: To help students learn that words are made of discrete sounds and to help them identify those sounds, you have to pronounce all the sounds in words, and you have to pronounce them correctly. Along with this, you want to avoid adding extra sounds or leaving out sounds. Your enunciation must be clear and correct.

Much of phonemic awareness stems from the ability to say the sounds in words. Students who can accurately pronounce words will have an easier time learning this skill. On the other hand, students learn to say new words based on what they hear. If they hear the correct pronunciation, they learn to use correct pronunciation, and that translates into correctly finding the sounds within words.

Many words sound similar, except for one or two sounds. For example, "lightning" and "lightening" are different by only one sound. Unless students hear each word correctly, they may have difficulty distinguishing one from the other. Other words differ only based on emphasis, such as deCREASE (the noun) and DEcrease (the verb). The list of commonly mispronounced words is long, including "arctic" (not "artic"), "supposedly" (not "supposably"), "height" (not "heighth"), "correct" (not "correck"), and "jewelry" (not "jewlery").

Your enunciation will become especially important as students begin to move from phonemic awareness to phonics, as they try to match up sounds with symbols (letters), which is necessary for learning to read. Phonics and word recognition will be simpler if the letters correspond to the sounds students are accustomed to hearing. Correct pronunciation will also contribute to correct spelling. You are the model.

Unlike the other strategies described below, modeling is not the basis for learning activities. It is what you do all the time.

Q and A / Oral response: With this strategy, you ask students questions about sounds and they respond orally. Once you have selected the phonemes to study, you ask questions that require students to perform various sub-skills with those sounds.

For example, let's say you are teaching the "ow" sounds and the blending sub-skill. You can instruct students to say "ow" following your prompt, and then to combine your prompt with the "ow" sound. You say "c", the students say "ow", and together you say "cow." You say "h", the students say "ow", and together you say "how."

As another example, you can ask students to say the first sound in "how," and then ask what word they get if they change the "h" sound for a "k" sound: "cow." For a more challenging example, you can have students provide examples of words with the "ow" sound, such as "clown," "plow," "ouch."

The section "Continuum of Complexity: Skill Types" above has many similar examples of using this strategy. The point of this strategy is to provide students some type of direction or question that requires them to use one or more sub-skills to provide a response.

My recommendation is to have students work in small groups to first determine their answer and then to provide their response together.

Sound searching and identification: As students get older, they learn the names of more things. With younger children, you can ask them to find an object in the room that has a particular sound. With older children, you can ask them to find words that contain specific sounds in specific locations within the word. What they are doing is searching for examples of the sound and identifying where those sound are used. This strategy is also useful for expanding students' vocabulary.

A common (and fun!) activity for this strategy is the game I-Spy. When you are playing I-Spy to help students develop phonemic awareness, you need to ask most of the questions. You can let students ask some of the I-Spy questions, but by asking most of them yourself, you ensure that students get practice with the one or two target phonemes. For example, if you are focusing on the long "o" sound (as in "flow"), you can ask, "I spy something clear with the "o" sound" (window). As students make guesses, you can have them identify and count out the phonemes in the words to determine whether or not the word actually has the right sound. Then you might ask, "I spy something tall and brown that has the "o" sound" (door).

Rhyming poetry and songs: Young children like to sing, and they like hearing and repeating rhymes. Older students, too, enjoy rhyming poetry, especially as they learn more about rhythm and meter, although getting them to sing can be a challenge. Because children naturally enjoy rhyming poetry and songs, you can use them to practice a variety of phonemic awareness skills.

Rhyming poetry and songs help students to develop a sense of word sounds, matching sounds, emphasis, syllables, word groups, sentence structure, and pacing—all of which contribute to developing phonemic awareness skills.

They also form the basis for many fun instructional activities. For example, students can "high-five" each other for every rhyming word and they can hop forward towards a goal line for every syllable. You can have students create their own rhyming couplets using a word list of pairs of rhyming words.

Repetition and restructuring: "Repetition" means studying the same sounds many times over time. Once students demonstrate their ability to find certain sounds within words, you will move on to other sounds. However, from time to time, come back to those same sounds to ensure students retain their grasp of them. Not only will this reinforce their ability to identify those sounds but also it will provide students with a sense of accomplishment and progress that will encourage them to keep learning.

"Restructuring" means studying the same sounds through a

variety of phonemic awareness skills. For example, you might be focusing on the "-ite" sound at the end of words. Students can also study that sound within words, swap other sounds for the "-ite" sound, and find out what happens to words when you remove that sound.

The point is to explore sounds in a variety of ways. When you incorporate this strategy into your learning activities, students will improve their ability to break words apart into component sounds, put sounds together to make words, and perform the entire range of phonemic awareness skills.

We will visit repetition and restructuring again as we discuss strategies for learning vocabulary. As you will see, the concepts behind repetition and restructuring apply to both components of reading.

Phoneme / sound counting: To help students make that mental leap from whole words to sounds within words, have them count all the sounds they hear. They can do this by clapping their hands, making marks on a paper, or placing objects on a grid for every sound they hear. With more advanced students, you can have them circle letter combinations that produce individual sounds or that have beats in a rhythm.

Regardless of how students do it, the act of counting sounds they hear forces them to think critically about the phonemes within words. Then, as they improve their ability to identify individual sounds, they can begin learning more advanced phonemic awareness skills.

Sample Activities for Phonemic Awareness

Strategy	Sample Activity Types	Phonemic Awareness Sub-skills
Modeling	Continuous exposure by the teacher or other adults	Identification
		Blending
		Differentiation
		Isolation

Question and Answer / Oral Response	Short-answer questions	All sub-skills
	Explicit instruction	
	Call-and-response	
	Finding rhymes	
	Pair response to questions	
	Pair blending	
	Fill in missing words (based on a rhyme)	
	Teacher-led oral practice	
Sound Searching and Identification	Sounding out words	Identification
	I-Spy	Completion
	Identifying words by sounds	Differentiation
		Matching
	Creating rhymes	
	Word-grouping	
	Matching pictures to words	
Rhyming Poetry and Songs	Sing-along	Identification
	Fill in the missing words / line	Completion
	Hand clapping	Manipulation
		Matching
	Word swapping	
	Exaggerated recitation	

	Sound marking	
	Alphabet song	
Repetition and Restructuring	Any instructional strategies as you teach and reinforce the sub-skills	All sub-skills
Phoneme / Sound Counting	Sound boards	Identification
	Sound removal	Completion
	Marking written poetry	Deletion
	Clapping sounds / syllables	Isolation
		Matching
	Word grouping by sound counts	Reversal
	Matching words by sounds	
	Metered poetry	
	Letter bingo	
	Sound picture charts	

What Does Not Work for Phonemic Awareness Instruction

With so many sub-skills and potentially effective strategies, it might seem that just about anything you do will help students develop their phonemic awareness skills. This is not true. Some strategies, and associated activities, either do not contribute to phonemic awareness or are only minimally effective.

Strategy	Reason Why It Does Not Work
Flash Cards	When using flash cards, the emphasis is on decoding the words and word recognition. This is phonics, not phonemic awareness, and does not require identification and modification of the sounds within words.
Reading Drills	For the same reason as flash cards, reading drills do not require the use of phonemic awareness skills. Instead, the focus is on accurate decoding.
Sustained Silent Reading (SSR)	Phonemic awareness is about sound. SSR is silent. Students do not have to use any phonemic awareness skills when doing SSR.
Computerized Instruction	Very few computerized instructional programs recognize and analyze speech patterns. (Rosetta Stone comes to mind.) As a result, most programs cannot determine whether or not students are accurately identifying sounds or using phonemic awareness sub-skills. Some programs ask students to find a picture of an object with a particular sound in its name, similar to an I-Spy game. What they lack, however, is follow-up correction and instruction. These types of computerized instruction cannot be as effective as a teacher's instruction.
Worksheets	Worksheets might be used for assessment purposes if students are indicating letter groups, words, or pictures that have particular sounds. Of course, this assumes that students are already reading or already know the names of the items in the pictures, as well as the sounds within the words or names.

For instructional purposes, however, they are ineffective or, at the most, minimally effective. Worksheets are a very poor way to teach sounds or the phonemic awareness sub-skills.

Individual Oral Reading

Here, individual oral reading refers to a student reading aloud a passage without teacher intervention except, possibly, help with some of the words. Generally, with oral reading the focus is on phonics and fluency. It may be a decent strategy for assessing these two reading components, but simply reading words aloud does not help students learn to identify sounds within words or to modify them. Guided oral reading (and other out-loud reading activities with correction, instruction, and repeated reading), on the other hand, will give the teacher the opportunity to explore the sounds within specific words. Guided oral reading by itself does not provide instruction in phonemic awareness, but it can provide opportunities for phonemic awareness instruction.

Companion Reading Components

Phonemic awareness skills are best taught when combined with instruction in the following three reading components. As you are helping students learn phonemic awareness skills, also provide instruction in these components.

Phonics: Phonemic awareness skills contribute to phonics skills. They both relate to the sounds of, and within, words. Whereas phonemic awareness only addresses the sounds of words, phonics addresses the process of translating letters into sounds. Once students begin understanding letter sounds, probably around age four, you can begin teaching phonics. At that point, you can begin connecting the sounds within words to the sounds represented by letters. From that point on, help students understand the connection between the sounds they hear and the letters that represent them.

Vocabulary: Knowing how to pronounce words, and knowing the sounds within words, is not enough. Students also need to know what those words mean and how they are used. That is vocabulary. By including vocabulary development into your phonemic awareness lessons, you give students an overall better ability to understand what they hear and read.

Oral Language Development: To find sounds within words, to find words with similar sounds, and for all the phonemic awareness sub-skills, students need to know how words are pronounced! Pronunciation depends on context, setting, and culture—which means oral language development. Often, words are not pronounced according to their spelling, or even according to the standard pronunciation. For example, do you say "buddah" or "budder" or "butter"? As students begin transferring phonemic awareness skills to vocabulary and phonics, they need to understand that words can be pronounced in different ways, although there is a standard way. This is the realm of oral language development. Phonemic awareness skills will make more sense if you provide corresponding instruction in oral language skills.

Chapter 6
Phonics

Without phonics, words on a page are meaningless symbols. With phonics, symbols become words that students can understand and interpret. Without phonics, there is no reading. With phonics, all the other reading skills become possible.

Definition

The ability to transform written symbols into sounds.

Another term for phonics is "decoding." Letters on a page are a form of symbolic code, and "decoding" means understanding that code. A student who can break that code is able to sound out the letters and create spoken words. When you look at text and read it aloud, you are decoding. Even when you read silently, you are hearing the words in your head. You are doing phonics.

However, before phonics can make any sense at all, students must have some skill in phonemic awareness. Students must have some understanding that words are made of individual sounds before they can begin learning how those sounds are represented by letters.

Breaking Down Phonics Skills

Like all other reading components, phonics is not a single skill. Phonics is three skills, which together you use to turn written symbols into sound.

Synthetic phonics: producing the sound for each letter or letter combination and then blending those sounds into words. (a.k.a. "Blending") Example: Say the sounds for "D", "O", "R"; now put them together to make a word.

Analogous phonics: using knowledge of how letter combinations sound in a known word to help decode a new word. (a.k.a. "Comparing") Example: If you already know how to pronounce "ower" in "flower," then you know that "power" likely has a similar pronunciation because it has the same "ower" combination.

Analytical phonics: memorizing what sounds are associated with various letter combinations in words, and then analyzing words to find those letter–sound associations. (a.k.a. "Remembering") Example: Analyze the word "sleep" for letter–sound associations, remembering that the sound for the "sl" letter combination, the long-e sound of the "ee" combination, and the sound of the "p" letter.

Explaining These Sub-skills

Synthetic phonics: "Synthesize" means combining parts into a whole thing. With synthetic phonics, you synthesize the individual sounds into whole words. Students learning this skill will produce the sounds for individual letters and digraphs (two letters that combine into a single sound, such as "th"). Students focus on the parts of words and blend them together into whole words. Generally, this is the first phonics skill students begin to learn.

Students start by learning sounds that correspond to letters in the alphabet, and then they begin learning to decode very simple words that have one sound for each letter, which they can blend into a whole word. Once students learn the "k" sound for "C", the "uh" sound of "U", and the "p" sound made by the letter "P", they can sound out each letter in "cup", and synthesize those sounds into a whole word.

Analogous phonics: "Analogy" means comparing something you do not understand to something you already understand. When you recognize how they are similar, you can begin to understand the new thing. With analogous phonics, you recognize a familiar letter combinations in a new word, one that you already know how to pronounce. Then, you use that knowledge to help you decode the new, unfamiliar word.

Students learn this skill through clusters of words have similar letter patterns and combinations, such as "fall," "ball," "call," and "wall." Once they have learned to pronounce the sound of "all" in the word "fall," they can quickly learn to decode new words with the "all" letter combination because they only need to decode the new letters.

Analytical phonics: "Analytical" means examining something new and then breaking it down into recognizable parts. This is the opposite of synthetic phonics because students start with the whole word and then analyze the parts for letter–sound associations they have been taught.

Analytical phonics is necessary when the sounds for the individual letters cannot be synthesized into the correct sound. For example, the sounds of the letters "I", "G", "H", and "T" in "right" cannot be blended into the "ite" sound; you have to memorize the way they sound when written together.

Integrated Use of the Phonics Sub-skills

Phonics experts debate whether synthetic or analytical phonics are better, with research data suggesting that synthetic phonics may be more useful for most students. Experts who take this approach say that instead of tackling whole words, students should focus on letter sounds and blending them together. One argument they make is that the English language has too many sounds and too many ways to represent those sounds in writing. Trying to memorize them all (the analytic approach) is going to be unnecessarily difficult. And this is likely true.

But what they fail to recognize (or admit) is that even with the synthetic approach, you skill have to memorize that certain letters and letter combinations are pronounced in certain ways, which is more in line with the analytic approach.

And then there is the second sub-skill: analogous phonics. It looks like a combination of synthetic and analytical phonics: take a word, break it into known and unknown parts, and then blend those parts together.

The truth is that each of these sub-skills requires a different set of mental processes, each sub-skill contributes to the other two, and good readers use all three. We help students become strong readers by giving them guidance and practice in all three skills.

For synthetic phonics: you break new words into letters and letter combinations you have memorized (analytic), compare combinations with other words (analogous) for clues on how they sound, and then blend the sounds of those parts into a word (synthesis).

For analogous phonics: you recognize letter combinations within words (analytic), recall other words with that combination and how those words are pronounced (analogous), and then you blend the sounds of the letter pattern with any other letters or letter combinations in the word (synthesis).

For analytical phonics: you study a whole word (analytical), remember the sounds associated with certain letters and letter combinations learned from other words (analogous), recall the sounds of any additional letters and letter combinations, then blend them together into words (synthesis).

As you begin to think about designing instructional activities for phonics, remember that students need all three skills and incorporate them into the activities: sounding out and blending, finding similarities with other words, and applying direct instruction and memorized patterns to study whole words.

Principles for Phonics Instruction

I often describe phonics and phonemic awareness as two sides of the same coin. These two reading components require similar mental processes, although phonics includes the additional element of letter–sound associations. As evidence of the close ties between phonics and phonemic awareness, reading research and success with our reading programs indicate that both reading components rely on the same instructional principles.

Because your brain does similar things with phonics as it does with phonemic awareness, and because a student's brain grasps concepts of phonics and phonemic awareness through similar processes, the same principles will guide effective instruction in both components.

We will look at instructional strategies next, but all effective strategies and instructional activities are based on the same four principles, as follows.

1. Instruction needs to be explicit and systematic.
2. Instruction should focus on only one or two letter–sound associations at a time.
3. Instruction follows a "continuum of complexity."
4. Instruction needs to combine practice with application.

For a more comprehensive explanation of the first three principles, go back and read the principles of instruction for phonemic awareness again. I will discuss them briefly here as a reminder.

Explicit and Systematic Instruction

"Explicit" means you determine particular letter–sound associations to study. Rather than simply wrestling with decoding troublesome words when students stumble across them and then moving on, you plan instructional activities to target specific relationships.

"Systematic" means you have a plan. Once students master the letter–sound associations you are teaching them now, you already know what you will teach them next. To guide your "system," refer to the continuum of complexity.

One or Two Letter–sound Associations at a Time

This principle is fairly self-explanatory: determine what letter–sound associations students need to learn, and then focus instruction on the next one or two only. Use the continuum of complexity to determine next steps in learning, select one or two relationships to study within the current level of complexity or the next level, and then design instructional activities to teach them explicitly.

If you try to teach more than a few at a time, students will struggle to learn them. However, when you focus on one or two, and when you let students practice them repeatedly, their brains will develop strong neurological pathways, a form of "mental muscle memory." They will be able to use those skills naturally and without conscious effort. This is how students develop automaticity, i.e., mastery.

Combine Practice with Application

The various instructional strategies described below will help you design effective instructional opportunities for students to master the letter–sound associations. They will help students learn to recognize letter and letter combinations and turn them into sounds. But that is not enough.

Students need to put their fledgling skills into practice... immediately.

This means applying the instruction to real, meaningful text. No reading skill is useful until it is applied to meaningful text. Similarly, students strengthen their new skills by using them with text. In this way, students have both a purpose for learning phonics skills and an opportunity to practice those skills.

Does this mean that students will be able to "read" everything that is appropriate for their grade level or age? Of course not. But neither should they wait to read real text until they have mastered all of the phonics skills. As students begin to learn phonics skills, at any level, they need to see how they can apply those skills and how those letter–sound associations are used in text—whether or not they can read the entire text independently.

Following this instructional principle, you will engage students in activities that focus on phonics skills, followed by activities using meaningful text, followed by phonics skills again, followed by text again, followed by.... Back and forth, higher and higher.

Continuum of Complexity

Some phonics skills are easier for students to grasp than others, and some letter combinations are easier to decode than others.

In general, single-letter sounds are less complex than sounds made from multiple letters. Blends are less complex than digraphs, and digraphs are generally less complex than trigraphs.

Do not assume that students at a certain age or grade already understand simple skills or that they are ready for more complex skills. Start with the easy skills and move up the continuum until you reach skills that challenge students. In this way, you help students develop the foundational skills they need to understand more complex letter–sound associations.

The list below demonstrates the typical continuum of skills, from simple to complex. This is a general guide that reflects phonics skills from most simple to most complex.

Students may be at different places on the continuum, and they may find higher skills (though not much higher) easier to grasp than lower skills depending on their level of exposure to text and prior instruction. Because of these issues, students may progress through these skills differently than they are represented here. Regardless, this is a good general continuum.

Most Simple to Most Complex

- Naming the letters of the alphabet
- Producing the most common sounds for each letter beginning with the short sounds of vowels and consonants
- Recognizing and writing single letter–single sound associations
- Producing less common sounds and long sounds for vowels
- Recognizing and writing common V-C and C-V words (example: "to," "at")
- Recognizing and writing common C-V-C words (example:

"bug")

- Recognizing and writing common consonant digraphs (example: "sh," "th")
- Recognizing and writing common C-V-C-C words (example: "lamp")
- Changing letters in simple words to produce new words (example: "car" to "far")
- Recognizing and writing common digraphs that produce the same sound (example: the "sh" sound in "motion" and "shop")
- Using known letter combinations to blend sounds into new words through word clusters (example: "BL-ank," "BL-ow," "BL-ack")
- Recognizing and writing vowel digraphs with repeated vowels that produce single sounds (example: "ee," "oo")
- Recognizing and writing vowel digraphs of different vowels that produce single sound (example: "bean," "hair")
- Recognizing and writing less common multi-letter letter combinations that produce single sounds (example: "ough")
- Recognizing and writing less common digraphs that do not produce the sounds of the letters (example: "knife")
- Breaking multi-syllabic words into syllables and sounding out, then blending the syllables
- Recognizing and writing various ways that phonemes can be written (example: "door," "four," "more")
- Recognizing patterns for when vowels are produced by long or short vowel sounds (example: "ape" vs. "always")
- Recognizing the sounds of Greek and Latin roots in words
- Producing the sounds of non-English letter–sound associations (example: "foyer," "ciao")

What Works for Phonics Instruction

As just described under instructional principles, you want students to go back and forth between direct instruction and application. The first four strategies listed below focus on direct instruction of phonics skills.

Six Sample Strategies for Teaching Phonics

- Word clusters
- Sight words and phonics
- Matching words with meanings
- Word analysis
- Guided oral reading
- Writing

Word clusters: As with word clusters for phonemic awareness, students study, compare, contrast, sound out, blend, etc. words with similar letter–sound associations. Because children generally begin learning to identify rhymes long before they begin decoding, you will likely begin with simple words that rhyme, such as "car," "jar," and "far." Many words in these simple sets are known as C-V-C words, meaning Consonant-Vowel-Consonant.

As students begin to grasp those simple words, you may begin to work with clusters of words that have similar starting sounds, then middle sounds. Following the continuum of complexity, you will eventually introduce clusters of words with similar sounding digraphs and trigraphs, and with silent letters. Then, you and the students will move to clusters of words that have same sounds but very different letter combinations to produce those sounds, such as "laid," "played," and "grade."

Sight words and phonics: Sight words and phonics are related, but they are not the same.

With sight words, students are taught to automatically recognize whole words, meaning they memorize and can recall that a certain set of letters makes the sound of a particular word. Instruction in sight words, typically some type of recall drill, does help students develop automaticity in word recognition, and it can contribute to reading text. But it still isn't phonics.

Rather, with phonics, students are learning to decode—to sound out words. This is different than whole word recognition.

The point, however, is that although sight words and phonics are different, students will benefit from both and instruction should include both.

Matching words with meanings: Many students can sound out words in text but have no idea what the text passage is about. I call these students "word callers." They can perform decoding and call out the words, but they do not have any idea what those words mean. This is frustrating for students and does not lead to reading comprehension. The missing pieces are vocabulary knowledge and, to some degree, comprehension (but mainly vocabulary). Decoding is only useful if children know the meanings of words they are decoding!

With this strategy, students study the meanings of words that they are decoding. Obviously, most simple words do not need any vocabulary instruction. However, as students begin to encounter more advanced words or words that are related to various topics or school subjects, they will need vocabulary instruction to help them understand what they are reading when they find those words in text.

Word analysis: Some words are long and complicated, but if we study them, we see that they have parts we already know. Rather than being intimidated by those long words, we often find we need only to figure out the unfamiliar parts. Strong readers do this automatically, but younger or weak readers need help separating the known and unknown parts.

Many children look over a piece of text and say, "This is too hard!" We cannot let children say—or think—that. When children feel intimidated by text they have been asked to read, they will have an emotional reaction that will limit their ability to learn. (See chapter 1, section 6: "Create a safe environment" for more about emotions and learning.)

As the teacher, your job is to help students learn the habit of finding the parts they already know. Then, you help them sound out the new parts. Sometimes, the familiar parts are one- or two-letter combinations, but very often they are recognizable patterns, such as "tion" or "ough." For example, the word "thoroughness" is a tough word, but when we analyze the word, we see that it has a couple of common patterns "ough" and "ness." The new part is "thor." Once students sound out that part, they can blend all three parts together to say the entire word. They may surprise themselves by being able to read such big words.

Guided oral reading: Guided oral reading is one of those across-the-board great instructional strategies. It is useful for oral language, phonics, fluency, comprehension, and vocabulary. Although there are several ways to do guided oral reading, it generally looks like this for phonics.

1. The student reads aloud to the teacher (or another student), who is listening and reading along silently.
2. The teacher makes note of any words on which the student stumbles or demonstrates difficulty with decoding.
3. Once the student finishes reading the passage, the teacher helps the student sound out the troublesome words, and together they study those words through decoding and blending.
4. The teacher and student may read the passage aloud together a few times.
5. Once the student can correctly decode those words, the student attempts to read the passage aloud again.

By carefully selecting text passages that use the various letter–sound associations being studied, the teacher helps students apply the direct instruction to meaningful text.

Students enjoy this strategy because it gives them an opportunity to keep trying until they get it right. If you provide sufficient time to activities that use this strategy, students will succeed.

Writing: Writing is not reading, but writing can help students develop their phonics skills. If you recall from the continuum of phonics skills, most of the skills include "recognizing and writing." These two skills are closely related. With recognizing, students turn text into spoken words; with writing they turn spoken words into text. In both cases, students are using and practicing letter–sound associations.

Writing activities do not automatically help students improve their phonics skill. On the other hand, they give students opportunities to practice and refine their skills. They also give you the opportunity to identify letter combinations that may be difficult for the student and to provide instruction. When a student asks, "How do you spell [some word]?" your first response can be "What sounds do you hear?" followed by "And what letters can spell those sounds?" Keep track of those letter–sound associations that cause difficulties. You can use them for further instruction.

Sample Activities for Phonics

Strategy	Sample Activity Types	Phonics Sub-skills
Word Clusters	Finding rhymes / Rhyming poetry	Synthetic
		Analogous
	I-Spy	
	Quick erase / swap	
	Odd word out	
	Word searches in text	
Sight Words and Phonics	Sound timelines	All sub-skills
	Flash cards	
	Identifying site words in text (circle, clap on words, etc.)	
	Sound timelines	
	Call-and-response blending	
Matching Words with Meanings	Word analysis for roots	Analogous
		Analytical
	Graphic organizers	
	Vocabulary substitution	
	Vocabulary study prior to reading	

Guided Oral Reading	Guided oral reading	All sub-skills
	Choral reading	
Word Analysis	Syllabification	Synthetic
	Sound searching	Analytical
	Word grouping by letter combinations	
	Call-and-response blending	
	Quick erase/swap	
Writing	Rhyming Poetry	Analytical
	Journaling	

What Does Not Work for Phonics Instruction

Many activities used for phonics instruction either do not address phonics or are, at best, minimally effective. Following are common types of ineffective instructional activities for phonics. My recommendation: avoid them.

Strategy	Reason Why It Does Not Work
Incidental Instruction	The research is clear: systematic and explicit instruction works; incidental instruction does not. You have to know what you need to teach, and you have to focus on the phonics skills rather than wait for students to make a mistake and then address the problem.

Reading Drills / Flash Card Speed Drills	Flash cards have their place in phonics instruction, particularly for analytical phonics and developing word recognition automaticity. However, timing students and counting the number of correct or incorrect words is not instruction. It is assessment, and it sets up students for failure.
Sustained Silent Reading (SSR)	SSR does not require students to turn text into sound, so it does not require phonics. It might help strengthen existing skills by increasing familiarity with words, but it certainly is not instructional.
Computerized Instruction	I will call this one a "maybe." Computerized instruction may include asking students to click on the word they hear (speech to words) or to identify words that have/do not have certain sounds. On the other hand, it does not address the primary phonics skill, which is decoding text: accurately reading words aloud.
Round Robin Reading	Round robin reading is having students reading aloud one at a time. The first student reads the first part, and then the next student reads the next part, and so forth. In addition to being a frustrating and painful experience for weak readers, round robin reading does not provide any instruction in the phonics sub-skills. Do small-group guided oral reading instead.
Worksheets	Another "maybe." In general, worksheets are not a useful tool for helping students sound out words, though they might be useful for helping students identify words with particular sounds or within a word cluster. They might increase familiarity with groups of words, but they do not address the primary phonics skill, which is decoding text.

Companion Reading Components

Phonics skills are best taught when combined with instruction in the following three reading components. As you are helping students learn phonics skills, also provide instruction in these components.

Phonemic Awareness: Phonemic awareness skills contribute to phonics skills. Both reading components relate to the sounds within words. Whereas phonemic awareness only addresses the sounds in words, phonics addresses the letter–sound associations that students need for decoding. To grasp phonics and build their phonics skills, students have to be able to identify sounds in words.

Vocabulary: In the subsection above on matching words to meanings, I discussed how phonics is worthless if students do not know the meanings of words they read. Indeed, phonics only helps students read if they know the meanings of words. Provide instruction in vocabulary while providing instruction in phonics—do both at the same time. Help students learn what words mean as they study specific sound–letter associations. Then, as they read meaningful text, they will be able to decode the words and understand what the text.

Comprehension: Once students are able to decode the words, and once they understand what the words mean, they can begin to analyze the text itself. Saying the words aloud correctly is not enough to get to improved comprehension; they have to understand the meanings of words. Similarly, understanding the meanings of individual words is not sufficient. Now, they need to put it all together and study the text. This is when phonics finally becomes reading.

CHAPTER 7
FLUENCY

Fluency is a skill that strong readers have. However, fluency is not actually a reading skill by itself. Instead, it is a combination of three other reading components: phonics, comprehension, and oral language.

Definition

> The ability to read aloud accurately with appropriate expression and pace.

Reading aloud accurately means a student speaks the actual words in the text. The student does not say a different word, does not say the word incorrectly, does not skip words, and neither adds nor subtracts from the written word. For example, if the word in text is "bountiful," the student does not say "beautiful," "bounty," and etc. A student must accurately decode or recognize the word to say it aloud accurately—i.e., phonics.

Reading aloud with appropriate expression means the student modifies his or her tone of voice, volume, pausing, etc. to match the context of the text. The context of the text is important here because it reflects the intention of the author or characters. One way to think about this is to ask, "How would the author or character say this?" Expression relates to both fiction and nonfiction texts, but it is fairly subjective. Regardless, a student must understand the text to say it aloud with appropriate expression—i.e., comprehension.

Reading aloud with appropriate pace means the student reads at a generally acceptable pace based on both the content of the text and the norms of his or her culture. It also means that the listener can understand the words being spoken. A student must have good understanding of those norms and expectations to determine the appropriate pace for reading aloud—i.e., oral language.

Fluency does not have specific sub-skills, unlike the other reading components. This is mainly because fluency is not a separate reading skill. As you can see, each part of the definition of fluency relates to other reading components, and a reader with good fluency has skills in those other components.

Three Types of Oral Readers

There are three broad types of oral readers: too slow, too fast, and just right.

The "too slow" readers generally are trying to decode each word as they read aloud, and they may need to try more than once to read some of the words. "Too slow" readers focus on decoding skills. "Too fast" readers are trying to show you how quickly they can decode and speak the words. They may skip or incorrectly decode some words, but they keep racing along. Their focus, too, is reading aloud individual words.

If you ask either type of reader to explain or interpret what they have just read, very likely they will not be able to tell you. They have focused on individual words and not what those words mean when you put them all together. The "too slow" reader probably needs a lot of help with decoding skills. The "too fast" reader probably needs a lot of help with comprehension and pacing. Regardless, neither one is fluent. They have not read aloud accurately and with correct expression and with correct pacing. To be fluent, a reader needs to do all three.

The "just right" reader does all three. Strong readers read aloud "just right." If you ask the "just right" reader to explain or interpret the text, he or she will likely be able to do it. At a minimum, the "just right" reader will be able to ask questions about the text that indicate he or she has a basic understanding of the content, though the concepts or information may yet be confusing.

With well-designed fluency activities that address decoding, comprehension, and oral language skills, the "too slow" and "too fast" readers can become "just right" readers.

When the National Reading Panel discussed fluency, they noted that it is something that strong readers can do as a result of having strong skills in other areas. So, if fluency is only a combination of other skills and is not a specific skill by itself, why teach it?

Why Teach Fluency

You do not actually "teach" fluency: you teach students skills in those other three areas. When you do fluency activities, you are teaching skills in phonics, comprehension, and oral language. "Teaching fluency" means activities that allow students to practice and demonstrate their skills in phonics, comprehension, and oral language by reading aloud.

As it turns out, there are several excellent reasons for specifically including fluency activities in your reading instruction.

1. As noted, fluency activities give students opportunities to practice their decoding/word recognition skills, comprehension strategies, and oral language using meaningful text. I will describe effective fluency activities below: they are very good for practice. They help students strengthen their existing skills and provide opportunities to expand on those skills.

2. Also as noted, fluency activities give students the opportunity to demonstrate their skills in decoding, comprehension, and oral language. This means that you, the teacher, can gauge how well students are decoding and interpreting the text. Fluency activities are a natural assessment, and you can use that information to make instructional plans.

Three Misconceptions about Fluency Instruction

1. *Flash cards help with fluency.* Often, what is described as fluency instruction is actually word recognition, which is phonics. Reading individual words on flash cards accurately is not fluency. You cannot become or demonstrate fluency unless you are reading actual text as opposed to sample phrases or single words. To be fluent, you need to demonstrate all three parts of the definition: accuracy, expression, and pace. You need to read meaningful text.

2. *Fluent readers read fast.* Being able to read aloud fast, even if accurately, is not fluency. Being able to read quickly might be a sign of good word recognition and decoding, but that is only part of the definition for fluency. Additionally, it can promote the idea that the point of reading is to get through it as quickly as possible. It isn't. The point of reading is to understand and make use of what we read.

3. *Fluency requires 100% accuracy.* It is possible to be fluent and still not have 100% accuracy in reading aloud, particularly if you are reading a sample of text for the first time. With practice on a single piece of text, you can attain 100% accuracy, but you might not have perfect accuracy when you first read aloud a new piece of text. Measuring a student's accuracy on the first attempt, or giving students only one chance, sets up that student for failure. A better expectation is improvement over time.

Principles for Fluency Instruction

The way you go about helping students to develop their fluency skills will determine whether students become more confident about reading or less. Many people are nervous about speaking in front of groups, and asking students to read aloud in front of their peers can provoke the same feelings of dread. This is especially true for students who are already struggling to read and who do not want to be perceived as stupid by their classmates. Students may be confident to read aloud solo later after they have practiced within a small group.

Conversely, if you follow these principles for instruction, you will mitigate the emotional barriers that can prevent students from progressing, and you can help students become stronger, more confident readers.

We will look at instructional strategies next, but all effective strategies and instructional activities are based on the same four principles, as follows.

1. Instruction needs to allow multiple attempts.
2. Instruction needs to focus on small-group participation.
3. Instruction needs to use high-interest text.
4. Instruction needs to include feedback and correction.

Multiple Attempts

Providing multiple attempts means letting the student read the same piece of text aloud multiple times. It generally looks like this: read aloud, get correction, focus on fixing any issues, and read aloud again. Repeat as necessary. (You might recognize this as guided oral reading.)

Most students will make mistakes the first time they try to read something out loud. If they get only one chance, they will learn that (a) they are not good at reading aloud, (b) the teacher is more interested in finding faults than in helping them improve, and (c) only perfection is rewarded.

On the other hand, if students understand that they are expected to make mistakes the first time, then they do not have to worry about appearing incompetent. Any errors will not be held against them because they are going to get another chance. Each time a student reads the same piece of text aloud, he or she will get better at it. The student will build his or her skills, develop more confidence, and feel the pride of accomplishing something difficult. So many benefits!

Small-Group Participation

When students read aloud together, they feel safer, they can hear how their fellow students pronounce words, and they have an inherent desire to perform their best. They hear other students make mistakes and recognize that they are not alone in having difficulty. It promotes the ideas that the goal is improvement and that participation leads to learning. This mitigates nervousness, avoidance, and indifference to the task. It is also more fun.

Having students read together as a small group still allows you to provide individual feedback, and the group members can help point out words or phrases that were difficult. They will learn to assess themselves. Students can help one another work through those challenges and can make decisions about expression and pacing. They will work towards a group goal rather than simply trying to get it over with.

Rather than single out students to perform, have students work together. Students will make better progress in phonics, comprehension, and oral language.

High-interest Text

Using interesting text has several benefits. First, students will be interested in what they are reading, and they will want to know the content of the text. This gives them motivation to participate. Second, students are likely to have read something about the topic or other text in the genre. This means they will be more likely to know the vocabulary and recognize the words. Third, students will be more willing to read the text aloud multiple times.

Feedback and Correction

Generally, during the first oral reading of a text, students will make mistakes with decoding, expression, or pacing. They need someone to help them identify the challenging parts and to ask questions about the meaning of the text. They need someone to say, "Let's try this again." Most students will want to know how they did, which means you or other students tell them what went well and what needs improvement. That is feedback.

Once students receive feedback, they need help making corrections. This may be in the form of helping them sound out words or modeling how to read the text aloud. It may include assistance in understanding the content or help understanding how to modify the verbal expression. Basically, the teacher or other students help figure out how to decode the text correctly, how to provide appropriate expression, and how to modify the pacing.

Feedback and correction lead to improvement, and you provide both after each attempt at reading text aloud. Students will also appreciate knowing how they are improving.

What Works for Fluency Instruction

With the instructional principles just described, you can use a variety of strategies to help students develop their fluency. Any strategies you use need to address all three skill sets to meet the definition of fluency. Four proven strategies are listed below. Each of them will help students strengthen and combine their phonics, comprehension, and oral language skills, which means they are effective at helping develop fluency.

Four Sample Strategies for Teaching Fluency

- Guided oral reading
- Choral reading
- Echo reading
- Plays and skits

Guided oral reading: This is the top strategy for helping students develop fluency. It works very well for helping students improve their decoding skills, increase comprehension of the text, and understand how to express the text appropriately.

I described guided oral reading already in the "What Works for Phonics Instruction" section of the previous chapter, but here it is again, with a few additional comments that help tailor this strategy to fluency.

1. The student reads aloud to the teacher (or another student), who is listening and reading along silently.

2. The teacher makes note of any words on which the student stumbles or demonstrates difficulty with decoding.

3. Once the student finishes reading the passage, the teacher helps the student sound out the troublesome words, and

together they study those words.

4. New for Fluency: The teacher and student discuss the meanings of new words or words that the author may be using in an unfamiliar way. They also discuss the content using higher level questions.

5. The teacher and student may read the passage aloud together a few times, which may be followed by more discussion and questions about the content.

6. Once the student can correctly decode the troublesome words and demonstrate understanding of the content, the student attempts to read the passage aloud again. This is step one again, and the entire process may be repeated as needed.

As you can see, guided oral reading is a fairly comprehensive strategy that comprises many skills and activities. It is a top recommended strategy for helping students learn to read well.

Choral reading: Choral reading refers to students reading aloud in unison. In many ways, choral reading includes the same steps as guided oral reading, although the attention to individual student errors and the discussion steps may be more limited. However, the major difference between choral reading and guided oral reading is that choral reading is, by definition, a group strategy whereas guided oral reading can be either an individual or small group strategy. You can use choral reading with fiction or nonfiction text, prose or poetry, and dramatic or narrative content.

Choral reading provides three advantages that are not included in "normal" guided oral reading.

1. Students can participate in larger groups, even entire classrooms at once.

2. With larger groups, you can assign parts to groups of students (but never to individual students). For example, if you have students chorally read a play, several students together can read the words of various characters. For another example, you can have students "dramatically" read alternating lines in a poem.

3. Students can incorporate movement into the dramatic expression of the text, which not only increases participation but also gives students another way to analyze and demonstrate their understanding of the text.

For one more advantage, choral reading is useful for second-language learners to understand pacing, expression, and standard pronunciation of words in a safe, fun environment.

At the school where I used to teach many years ago, we held an annual choral reading competition among classrooms. These types of competitions are fairly common. Search YouTube for "Choral Reading Competition," and you will find some really great examples of what this can look like with your students.

Echo reading: As the name implies, first person reads the text aloud, and then a student reads the same text aloud. The first person can be the teacher or a student. Just make sure that the first person has good fluency. For the student, the value of echo reading is that the student has a role model for what the text should sound like when read aloud.

Many teachers combine echo reading with guided oral reading. As the first step of guided oral reading, the model for reading aloud gives students an understanding of what they are attempting to reproduce.

Plays and skits: Plays and skits have several benefits. They can involve larger groups of students. They require a good understanding of the content, especially character purpose and expression, and they require correct decoding in order to say the lines correctly. One recommendation: if you use plays and skits, make sure you have an audience other than the teacher. This way, it will be more meaningful and provide better motivation for participation and learning.

Using plays and skits to help students develop their fluency works well, but it can be quite time consuming, even if you do not have students try to memorize their parts.

Sample Activities for Fluency

The strategies for fluency already suggest instructional activities that you can use to help students develop their fluency. However, the sample activities listed below provide more detail about what these strategies may look like in action. You may notice that sub-skills are not listed in the following table, which is because fluency does not have sub-skills. On the other hand, each activity you design needs to address the decoding, comprehension, and oral language components of fluency. Each activity should also be designed to incorporate the four principles of fluency instruction.

Strategy	Sample Activity Types
Guided Oral Reading	Small group choral reading, with discussion of the content, feedback and correction, etc.
	Partner reading, with one partner serving as the "teacher", using a teacher-generated list of questions for discussion
	Close reading of brief passages integrated into guided oral reading
	Small group oral reading to an audio recorder for the group to analyze, make corrections, and record subsequent attempts
Choral Reading	Whole class dramatic oral reading of a poem
	Discussion on how to interpret the text, followed by choral reading
	Small groups reading aloud a summary they have written about a text
	Several small groups reading aloud a section of a larger text following practice (not knowing in advance which sections they will be assigned to read aloud)
Echo Reading	Two small groups of students reading aloud to one another, with the second group repeating the same section as the first group, followed by discussion regarding two groups' interpretations
	Teacher reading aloud, with all students repeating the text in the same manner; the teacher may intentionally use an inappropriate rate or expression to prompt discussion

Plays and Skits   This is self-explanatory. One note: if you use this strategy, let the students practice repeatedly and make sure they have an audience other than the teacher or classmates. Make it real!

What Does Not Work for Fluency Instruction

The definition of fluency, the principles for instruction, and the effective instructional strategies are quite clear about what you want students to do and how you can help them do it.

The following table describes three types of instructional strategies and activities that either do not align with the definition of fluency and principles or do not align with effective strategies.

Strategy	Reason Why It Does Not Work
Flash Cards	Think about the definition of fluency; it includes appropriate expression and pacing. Students can do neither one if they are looking at individual words or disconnected phrases on flash cards. Flash cards may have some value for word recognition but not for fluency.
Speed Drills & Timed Assessments	The point of reading (whether aloud or silently) is not to do it as fast as possible. Similarly, the point of fluency instruction is not to see how many words a student can decode correctly in a minute or two. These types of activities are assessment and not instruction, they only address the phonics component of fluency, and they lead to a misunderstanding of the purpose for reading aloud.

| Round Robin Reading | Round robin reading is students each taking a turn to read the next section of text, one student after the other. It has four major problems.

First, it typically does not include instruction, feedback, or correction. Nor does it allow a student multiple attempts to read the same passage. Even when the teacher does intervene to help a student struggling with pronunciation or decoding, the student re-attempts the word and then keeps going.

Second, only one student is participating at a time. The other students are supposed to be reading along silently, but there is no reason for them to do so. Round robin reading is called a group activity, but in reality, it is just one student at a time.

Third, round robin reading generally does not include discussion about the passage, expression, or pacing. If anything, students will want to get through their section as quickly as possible.

Fourth, and finally, round robin reading is painful for both the student who is put on the spot to read and for the other students who have to listen and pretend interest even if the student reading has poor fluency. |

Companion Reading Components

Because fluency is a combination of three reading components, any instruction in fluency has to specifically address those three areas: phonics, comprehension, and oral language. If the instruction does not address those areas, it is not fluency. To assist with these three components, also add vocabulary instruction.

Phonics: Phonics instruction helps students with accurate decoding, the first part of the definition for fluency. As students read aloud, they may struggle with decoding some of the words. As you pair fluency with phonics instruction, choose text that contains words with the target letter–sound associations you are studying with phonics instruction. The fluency activities, therefore, will provide students with practice in those target associations and give you the opportunity to assess whether students are mastering them.

Comprehension: Comprehension instruction helps students with the appropriate oral expression of the text, which is the second part of the definition for fluency. Throughout fluency instruction, have students engage in activities that help them understand the text. The opposite is also true: as students are engaging in comprehension activities, include fluency activities. As noted previously, effective strategies for fluency include analysis and discussion of the text, which leads to comprehension.

Oral Language: Oral language helps students with the pacing for reading aloud and, to some degree, the expression, which is the third part of the definition for fluency. Oral language includes the study of how language is used appropriately, and this includes appropriate expression and pacing. As students are trying to figure out how to speak the text, you are really engaging in oral language.

Vocabulary: Vocabulary instruction fits very nicely into fluency activities. You will tie fluency instruction to vocabulary instruction by selecting text that has target words to learn. Also, through the discussion of the text, you will help students figure out what words mean. Ultimately, if students are going to understand what the text means, they have to know what the words mean. As you will see later in the vocabulary chapter, study new words first before students read them in text, whether silently or aloud.

Chapter 8
Vocabulary

Students cannot understand texts if they do not understand the words. The same is true when they are listening to people speak. On the flip side, they have to know the meanings of words to express their own ideas. When we talk about vocabulary, we ask "How many words does a student know?" From the standpoint of reading instruction, the definition of "vocabulary" is broader than how many words a student knows.

Definition

Ability to understand words as they are used in a text.

The phrase "as they are used in a text" is important to remember. As we saw in the discussion of oral language development, words can have many meanings. In vocabulary instruction, we want students to learn not only what words mean but also what they mean when the author uses them. Sometimes they are the same, but other times they are not.

This phrase also means that students need to learn how to understand and interpret words. Students, and all people, will encounter unfamiliar words or words used in unfamiliar ways. Vocabulary instruction also needs to help students figure out what new words mean and what the author intends to communicate by using them.

Students with good vocabulary skills not only know the meanings of many words but also know how to discover the meanings of words.

Breaking Down Vocabulary Skills

Now that we have applied the definition of "vocabulary" to reading instruction, we have a good idea about the various sub-skills of vocabulary development and use. The eight sub-skills are as follow.

Word application: using words appropriately according to their meaning and context (See the chapter on Oral Language

Development for more information about using words appropriately for the context.)

Meaning discovery: applying a learning process for discovering the meanings of new words found in a text (This sub-skill is the basis for the next six sub-skills that follow.)

Decoding: sounding out words

Word part knowledge: identifying and understanding components of words, typically prefixes, suffixes, and roots; understanding how words change for tense and person

Word replacement: identifying synonyms and antonyms for words

Word comparison: identifying other words that have similar parts or that fit the same grammatical usage

Content analysis: identifying the theme or topic of a passage, identifying words or phrases that provide clues about unfamiliar words

Definition research: finding a reliable source for the definitions of words; analyzing given definitions for their relevancy to the content

Explaining These Sub-skills

Word application: Word application has two parts. First, once the reader understands what the word means, the reader uses it multiple times. This increases familiarity with the word, leading to automaticity. Also, this is how new words found in text become part of a reader's oral vocabulary. Second, the reader considers how the word applies in different contexts and how the word may be used in different ways to communicate ideas. This is done through reading the word in multiple texts and through hearing and using the word in different situations.

With word application, the reader learns to use the new words. In fact, the various sub-skills are only valuable when they lead to word application.

Meaning discovery: We cannot teach students every word they need to know. Students will always encounter new words while reading. The discovery process is how strong readers learn the meanings of unfamiliar words. It is a multi-step process that starts with decoding, continues to word analysis and analysis of context clues, and may require research. When students learn the discovery process, they will have the skills needed to understand new words they find and to expand their vocabulary on their own. The next section will discuss the discovery process in more detail.

The remaining sub-skills help students apply the meaning discovery process.

Decoding: Students, like all people, may misread words in text. They may read the word but think it is something else. This is actually quite common. For example, the text may use the word "assent" but the student reads "accent." Because the brain tries to force new information into existing patterns, a student may see an unfamiliar word and think it is a more common word. This will lead to confusion about the word and the passage as a whole.

Students may also encounter words that look unfamiliar but are actually known. Like most people, students tend to have a larger oral vocabulary than reading vocabulary. Oral vocabulary refers to words a student understands when he or she hears them; reading vocabulary refers to words that a student understands when he or she reads them. As a result, the student may see a word in text that looks unfamiliar but that he or she already knows.

In both cases, accurately sounding out the word will help students understand and use the word. If a student can recognize the word when it has been decoded, the student expands his reading vocabulary and understanding of the text passage.

Word part knowledge: Word part knowledge allows reader to find the meaningful parts within words, interpret the meaning of those parts, and then put all the meanings together to define a new word.

All words have a root form, which is the basic word once you strip away anything added to it, such as prefixes or suffixes. For example, the word "indefatigable" seems like a pretty complicated word. When we examine it, however, we see that it has the root word "fatigue" (not "fat"!) with two prefixes and one suffix added to it. The first step in word part knowledge is learning to identify the root word. Once the student does that, we start to look for any additions to the word that might affect its meaning. In this example, prefix "in" means "not";

When helping students analyze words, we ask them, "Do you recognize any parts in this word? Does anything look similar to what you have seen in other words? What do those parts mean when you use them in other words?" If they can figure out the parts, they can figure out the word.

Word comparison: This sub-skill is actually an extension of the word part knowledge skill. With word comparison, students consider words that have similar parts, such as similar suffixes or similar roots. By analyzing similar words, readers get clues about what the currently unfamiliar word means.

For example, consider "indefatigable" again. Think about other words that contain the suffix "-able", such as "eatable," "drinkable," and "navigable." In each case, the suffix "-able" indicates that something can be done or accomplished or that the action is possible. By thinking about how the suffix "-able" is used in similar words, we get a clue about how it applies to "indefatigable" and how it modifies the root word. What we are doing is comparing "indefatigable" to other words that have similar parts. Good readers do this naturally, but others may need to develop this habit.

To perform this mental task, students first must be able to identify the parts within words, which is word part knowledge.

Content analysis: Another way to describe this skill is "Context Clues," but what readers are actually doing is analyzing the content surrounding the new word. They first think about the overall topic of the passage or paragraph. The passage will be about one topic, and all the information and words in that passage will relate to the topic. The unfamiliar word, too, will likely be about that topic. That is the first clue.

Then readers think about key words and phrases in the passage. What are they about? What words are commonly used and what do they mean? The unfamiliar word will likely relate to those words. Finally, readers consider the sentence in which the word appears. The preceding text may indicate what information is being provided by the new word. I mentioned this before, but one way we figure out what the word may mean is to mentally blank it out. Once you do all the preceding steps, consider what word would make sense in the blank?

Using content analysis may not provide a specific definition of the word, but it does give readers a general sense of what the word might mean or what information it provides. In most cases, this is enough to make sense of the entire passage.

Definition research: When all else fails, look up the word online or in a dictionary. (I usually type "define ___" into an Internet search engine.) But looking up a definition is not sufficient. Most words have multiple meanings, and a reader has to choose the one that seems to fit the content best. Even a word as simple as "air" has more than five definitions. Which one is the right one?

To use the dictionary definition, several things must happen first: the reader must have an understanding of the content, the reader must figure out what part of speech the word is, and the reader must be able to identify parts within the words. In short, before being able to use a dictionary definition, the reader has to first conduct word part and content analyses.

The Word Discovery Process

What Strong Readers Do with New Words

When people with good reading skills encounter new words in text, they generally follow the same process for figuring out what those words mean. (This assumes, of course, that they do not skip over the words.) They follow a process of decoding and discovery. The process looks like this.

1. Attempt to decode the word.

    Readers try to sound out the word first to see whether or not they actually do know the word. After all, it is possible that they know the word but simply do not recognize it when written.

    If they know the word once they decode it, great! They keep reading. Otherwise, they go to the next step.

2. Analyze the word parts.

    Readers look for suffixes, prefixes, root words, parts of root words, etc., to try to find clues about the word meaning. For example, if they come across the word "aggrandize," they might recognize the root "grand," which means "big" and "important." They might also recognize the "ize" which means "to make something." Once they recognize those parts, they put them together to create "make something seem bigger or more important."

    Overall, if readers know what the parts mean, they can come up with a working definition of what the word as a whole means. Once they have done that, they sound out the entire word again (decoding) and keep reading. Otherwise, they go to the next step.

3. Examine the context.

Readers consider the entire passage in which the word occurs. They ask whether they understand the theme or topic of the passage. They look for key words or phrases that might explain the unfamiliar word. They mentally blank out the unfamiliar word and try to figure out what word or meaning would fill in the blank according to the passage.

If they think they know approximately what word or words might fit the context of the passage and what might fill in the blank, they read the entire passage with that filled-in information to see whether the passage still makes sense.

If the passage still makes sense, they do not keep reading. Instead, they re-examine the original word and see if they can now interpret the word parts. They ask themselves whether or not the possible definition fits any of the parts of the word (word analysis), they sound out the entire word (decoding), and then they keep reading. Otherwise, they go to the next step.

4. Look up a definition.

    If, and only if, all the previous steps failed to give them a sense of the word meaning, readers look up the definition. This is the last step in the process, not the first step! It might take a strong reader only seconds to get to this step, but that is not the point. The point is that strong readers try to figure out the meaning before they look up the word.

    Once strong readers have looked up a word, they do not keep reading. First, they have to make sure the definition fits the passage (examine the content), they see if the dictionary definition gives any clues about word parts (word analysis), they sound out the entire word (decoding), and then they keep reading.

This is the entire decoding and discovery process. As you can see, strong readers do not jump to any particular step. They go through the process. Neither do they keep reading once they have an idea about the meaning. They go back to prior steps and confirm their ideas.

What Weak Readers Do with New Words

Weak readers typically either skip the word, which means they may not understand the passage, or they jump to looking up the definition, which means they do not consider how the definition is supported by, or contributes to, the meaning of the entire passage. In both cases, they do not expand their vocabulary.

By following this process, good readers will learn new words and comprehend the text. How can weak readers get the same benefit? They learn to follow the decoding and discovery process.

Principles for Vocabulary Instruction

Students need to know a lot of words to become strong readers. Also, as described above, students need to know what to do when they encounter new words while reading. The principles for vocabulary instruction, if applied to your instruction, will help students with both needs.

If you will think for a moment about how very young children learn words, you will see that certain principles are in effect. For example, hearing certain words determines whether or not students will learn those words. If children hear a lot of words, they learn a lot of words. Unfortunately, the reverse is true, and many students enter school knowing fewer words than they will need.

These principles, therefore, are based on the processes for how people naturally acquire new words. As a teacher, your role is to make sure those processes are occurring. In our reading programs, we encouraged teachers to use strategies based on these principles for vocabulary instruction, and, as a result, students made significant gains in reading comprehension.

We will get to instructional strategies next. In the meantime, as you think about strategies and as you design instructional activities to help students develop their vocabulary, consider these five principles.

1. Instruction needs to increase students' exposure to words.
2. Instruction is both direct and incidental.
3. Instruction requires students to use new words.
4. Instruction promotes both recognition and analysis of new words.
5. Instruction is linked to real text.

Increase Students' Exposure to Words

This first and most important principle has a very important implication for you as the teacher, regardless of the students' ages: you have the responsibility to use a lot of words, use new words, use correct and accurate words, and use them repeatedly. When you repeatedly use new words, students will become familiar with them and will develop a deeper understanding what they mean and how they can be used.

We sometimes refer to "kid-friendly" language, meaning we use simple words that students already know. If we only use simple language, we will not increase students' exposure to new words, academic words, subject-specific words, or the multiple words that are available to describe things and concepts. We will not give them the words they need to understand what they hear and read or the words they can use to express their own ideas.

On the other hand, "kid-friendly" language does have its place in instruction. We can use simple language to help students understand new words and concepts. We use what they already know to help them learn something new. The point is to increase the number of new words that students hear, read, and have available to use. Do not be afraid to use new words with students. Use them, help students understand them, and keep using them.

This principle has another implication for instruction. To build a larger vocabulary, students need to read a wide variety of fiction and nonfiction texts. Young children, before they begin to read, need to hear a wide variety of stories and listen to information about many topics. By reading or hearing about many topics, both fiction and nonfiction, students will be exposed to a broad selection of words. Then, when they study unfamiliar words they read or hear, they learn new words that, over time, will become part of their oral and reading vocabularies.

Is this really true? Yes! Many research studies have shown that children who are exposed to a greater number of words develop stronger reading abilities, mainly because they understand the words in the texts.

Direct and Incidental Instruction

Direct instruction means the teacher has a plan for helping students learn specific words. With direct instruction, you decide what words you will expose students to, and then you engage students in activities to learn those words. Direct instruction works well if you know that students will encounter unfamiliar words in a text, need certain words for a subject or topic, and need better ways to explain their ideas. Generally, you help students become familiar with words, and then they encounter those words in text or discussion.

Incidental instruction is the opposite of direct instruction. With incidental instruction, students encounter unfamiliar words as they are reading, and you stop the reading to help them understand those words. This form of learning mimics what actually happens when people read: you are reading along happily and then run into a new word. With incidental instruction, that is the point where learning occurs. Generally, students encounter new words in text or discussion, and then you help them learn those words. Students will use the discovery process at this point. Keep track of those words and use them often in discussion.

Although both forms of instruction work, direct instruction may be better for helping students learn new words. However, incidental instruction is necessary because students need to know what to do when they find new words—and because you simply cannot plan for all the unfamiliar words they will encounter.

Require Students to Use New Words

Have you ever heard someone say, "Oh, I used to speak a little Spanish, but now I've forgotten most of it"? The same person may remember events from his or her childhood, including conversations and names. How can this be? A person can "forget" because the connection created within the brain is weak. The neural link within the brain that connects words to their meaning goes dormant. To prevent this from happening, the new information must be reinforced through sustained use.

The process of learning new words is no different. To ensure that students can understand, remember, and apply new words, provide them with sufficient opportunities to use those words. Once students have an introduction to a new word, subsequent reading instruction activities should provide opportunities (require) for students to keep using those words. Conversations with students, too, should provide opportunities and encouragement to use the new words. The more students use and encounter the new words, the better able they will be to remember what they mean.

Recognition and Analysis

The prior principle addressed remembering the meanings of new words. This is a little different here. By recognition, I am referring specifically to sight words: words that the student sees or hears and understands without having to think about them. These are words that have become a part of the student's oral vocabulary.

Another way to say this is "automaticity," meaning students can see or hear the word and automatically know what it means. For example, if I say "Maintenance staff dismantled my desk," you probably do not need to think about what I mean by "dismantled." You recognize the word and automatically know what I am talking about.

As an instructional principle, recognition refers to providing students with sufficient exposure through a wide variety of activities to help them automatically recognize and understand a word.

Analysis, on the other hand, means providing instructional opportunities that require a student to break words apart into meaningful parts, interpret how the parts influence the root word, and then put the parts back together to create a whole definition of the word. Analysis will include a study of prefixes, suffixes, etc., as well as a study of root words and their meanings. This is a process that good readers use, and it is one that all developing readers need to be taught. Instructional strategies, therefore, must accommodate and address the analysis process.

Link to Meaningful Text

Words are only important if they are used to communicate ideas. Additionally, you only know what a word is supposed to communicate when it is used in context, whether in speech or in text. Any study of vocabulary must be immediately applied to text or discussion. There is little point to learning new words if the learning is not applied to discussion and text. From the standpoint of reading instruction, students need opportunities to read the new words in text. Basically, we do not teach students a lot of words and then hope they will find them in text sometime later. Nor is there any reason to study words that students are not going to encounter, particularly in text.

The term "meaningful text" is also important to this instructional principle. Meaningful text does not include worksheets, flashcards, or similar artificial reading selections. It means text, both fiction and nonfiction, that has content of value, use, and interest. Bottom line: Students study words they will find in text, and vocabulary instruction needs to be integrated with actual reading.

> *With direct instruction:* study > read > study > read (etc.)

> *With incidental instruction:* read > study > read > study (etc.)

What Works for Vocabulary Instruction

The principles for vocabulary instruction give you the big ideas to consider when designing instructional activities. They reflect how people learn new words, from birth onward. These big ideas suggest that seven instructional strategies will be beneficial.

The seven strategies below are approaches for putting the principles into practice. The first two strategies are for you as the teacher. They are things that you can do, rather than what you want the student to do. You will use them all the time.

The next five strategies are types of activities that engage students in the normal, natural processes that all people use learn new words. Over time, you will use all the strategies. You may have other strategies that work, but these have proven to be effective.

Seven Strategies for Teaching Vocabulary

- Modeling
- Word wall (for the teacher)
- Study and apply
- Substitution
- Writing
- Self-defining
- Graphic organizers

Modeling: For the teachers and anyone else who wants to help students increase their vocabulary, use words that you want students to learn. Use them, maybe explain them or have students study them at first, but then keep using them. Use them when you talk to students, and use them when you write something that students will read. Continual exposure will lead to students' vocabulary development. Many words have more than one meaning, so also use them in a variety of ways. This will help students increase their knowledge of what the words mean and how they may be used to communicate different information.

Modeling is not a specific instructional activity, but it is a powerful strategy for helping students learn new words. Modeling new words is an essential strategy. No matter what else you do, do this!

Word wall: Many teachers use word walls: a list of vocabulary terms that is posted somewhere noticeable. Word walls help improve student familiarity with vocabulary terms, and they might help students remember how to spell them. For teaching students the meanings of words, however, they are very weak. They do not provide instruction, and they do not show students how words are used in text or speech.

To increase the instructional value of word walls, you could write sentences that use the words, or use completed graphic organizers. This would be better than simply listing the words.

From the standpoint of helping students increase their vocabulary, the best use of word walls is as a tool for the teacher. Word walls provide the teacher with a reminder to use the word, to find texts that use the word, and to develop specific instructional activities that build students' knowledge of the words. The word wall is not for the student but for the teacher! The strategy of using the word wall for teachers is a top recommended strategy.

Study and apply: Study and apply is the direct instruction approach to teaching vocabulary. Following this strategy, students study new words and then read them in text. Studying words before reading in text is shown to significantly help students improve their vocabulary and their comprehension of the text. You can use a wide variety of instructional activities for the "study" part of this strategy. Once students complete an activity, they should read text that contains those words.

You may pre-select the words. You may also have students skim through the text and find unfamiliar words. Study those words with a variety of activities, including using context clues from the passage in which they occur, and then read the text. Follow-up discussion about the text should encourage the students to use the words. This is a top recommended strategy.

Substitution: Many new words that students learn have similar meanings to words they already know. To help them learn and use the new words, have them switch the new word for one they already know. For example, if students are learning the word "fantasy," teach them that "fantasy" is similar to "make believe." When they read or hear fantasy, they can think of "make believe." This strategy uses synonyms as definitions for new words. It will help students remember the meanings of new words while improving their comprehension of what they read and hear. If you use this strategy, make sure students are using the new word, not the "easy" word in discussions and writing.

Writing: Students need practice using the new words. Although practice is often in the form of discussion, writing exercises also provide practice with new words. In fact, student writing is a great way for students to prepare for discussions about a text. Have them use the new words in their writing.

Using writing this way is far better than the typical "write a sentence using the word" type of activities. Making up sentences to use a word is a weak way to have students learn words. Isolated, invented sentences that use a new word do little to strengthen a student's understanding of what the word means and how it can be used. It might give you clues about a student's understanding, which makes it assessment, but it is not instructional. Instead, have students write their ideas, opinions, and knowledge about a topic. In this way, the writing actually has a purpose that contributes to reading comprehension while helping them learn to use new words.

Self-defining: Can you explain the meaning of "enjoy"? Can you explain it well enough (without using it) for another person to know what word you are describing? This is the basis of the self-defining strategy. Students create their own definitions for words and share them. They may compare their definitions to other students' definitions, and they may work with other students to create a common definition.

You will not use this strategy until after other types of activities for learning and using the words. Students need to learn something about the word first. Using this strategy makes students think carefully about the word meaning and its use, and it helps students improve their recognition and knowledge of the word.

Graphic Organizers: Graphic organizers are powerful tools for developing comprehension, and they work very well for vocabulary instruction, too. Graphic organizers help students collect information and categorize information about a word. They help students create a visual representation of information that can then become a mental framework for understanding and using the word. Students' (and everyone's) brains will try to do this naturally; the graphic organizer facilitates this process.

There are many types of graphic organizers and many ways to lay out information. A useful graphic organizer will include specific types of information:

- most commonly used dictionary definition,
- other definitions or uses for the word

- sample use of the word from a text students are reading or have read,
- parts of the word with meanings for those parts,
- synonyms and antonyms,
- part of speech, and
- and a sample from the student's writing.

The next page has an example that shows how a graphic organizer can depict information about a word. (I am sure you can design or find graphic organizers that are more attractive than this one.)

My writing:

Given definition:
Other meanings:

Word Parts
Part:
Means:

WORD

Word used in text:

Synonyms:
Antonyms:

Word Parts
Part:
Means:

Word Parts
Part:
Means:

Sample Activities for Vocabulary

You can do many types of instructional activities to help students develop their vocabulary knowledge. As long as you are addressing the principles for vocabulary instruction and using effective strategies, the activities will lead to improved vocabulary knowledge and reading comprehension. Sample activities to address the various strategies are below.

Strategy	Sample Activity Types	Vocabulary Sub-skills
Modeling	Continuous exposure by the teacher or other adults	Decoding
		Word part knowledge
		Word replacement
		Word application
Word Wall (as used by the teacher)	Continuous use by the teacher or other adults	Decoding
		Word part knowledge
		Word replacement
		Word application
Word Wall (with instructional content for student use)	Reference for other activities	Decoding
		Word part knowledge
		Word replacement
		Definition research

Study and Apply	New word search	All sub-skills
	Graphic organizers	
	Identifying context clues	
	Create-a-dictionary	
	Creating word categories	
	Visual representation	
Substitution	Word mapping	Word replacement
	Creating word categories	Word comparison
	Erase and replace	Definition research
	Definition mapping	Word application
	Word look-up	
	Create-a-dictionary	
	Call and response	
Writing	Journaling	Decoding
	Response to prompts	Word replacement
	Opinion essays	Content analysis
	Contrast / argument responses	Word application
Self-defining	Cards on head	Word replacement
	Create-a-dictionary	Word application
	Discussion	

Graphic Organizers	Partner graphic organizers	Decoding
	Create-a-dictionary	Word part knowledge
	New word search	Word replacement
		Definition research
		Word application

What Does Not Work for Vocabulary Instruction

As long as you are engaging students in recognizing words, analyzing word parts, reading and using new words, nearly all instructional activities will increase students' vocabulary. However, a few types of strategies are not effective, or are minimally effective.

Strategy	Reason Why It Does Not Work
Single or Short-term Use (words of the week)	To increase familiarity with new words and how they may be used correctly, students need a lot of exposure to and practice with the new words. Studying words for a few days and then leaving them will not provide the long-term exposure and use students need.
Single-sentence Writing	This strategy refers to activities in which students write a made-up sentence for a word. This is not instruction but assessment. Also, writing a single sentence or two that use the word does not provide meaningful, real use of the word for communication. It is artificial and does nearly nothing to help students understand what a word means and how it can be used. A better approach is to have the students write a reflection or summary of the text in which they use the new words.

Sustained Silent Reading (SSR)	Sustained silent reading may increase exposure to words, but for learning new words, it is minimally effective unless students know the discovery process. An interesting way to use SSR for vocabulary development is to have students keep a log of new words they find and then create a graphic organizer they can share. Students can also search for new words first, study them, and then read silently.
Oral Reading	Reading aloud does not increase vocabulary, although students may come across new words while reading. To use oral reading as a vocabulary exercise, have students first find new words and study them. Then, when reading aloud, students will understand the words and the text they are reading.
Computerized Instruction	Computerized instruction generally provides short-term exposure, study, and practice with words—not the long-term study that students need. It also doesn't provide broad-based exposure, such as in reading, discussion, or listening. Computerized instruction also generally does not provide the word analysis that students can use to figure out the meanings of words, and it certainly does not coach students through the discovery process. It might be useful as a supplement for live instruction, but it will never be as good.

Companion Reading Components

Vocabulary contributes to several other reading components, such as oral language, phonics, fluency, and comprehension. It goes both ways. If you are focusing on helping students develop their vocabulary, provide instructional activities in oral language, phonics, and comprehension that use the new words.

Oral language: Words can be used in many ways. With oral language instruction, students explore how word meanings change according to how they are being used. When oral language instruction is combined with vocabulary instruction, students study what the words mean according to an author and other ways the new words can be used. The result is an improved ability to understand and use words to communicate a variety of messages.

Phonics: Decoding is the first step in the process for learning new words and recognizing them in text. This has two implications for vocabulary instruction. First, students need to know how to decode words and have decoding skills that are sufficiently advanced for decoding the new words. Second, whenever students first encounter new words in text, or when they are using the discovery process for new words, they need to spend time decoding the words. Not only will this reinforce the first step in the discovery process but also will help students recognize the words when they find them in text.

Comprehension: Once students have a grasp of what a word means, they need to see how the word contributes to the meaning of a text passage. Learning words in isolation (without reading them in text or using them in discussion) has almost no value. Words must be applied. In terms of reading instruction, this means that students need to read the new words in meaningful text. As they do so, provide comprehension activities about the text. After all, the end goal of vocabulary instruction is not to learn new words. The end goal is to understand the text.

Chapter 9
Comprehension

Comprehension is the goal of reading programs, but it is much more than being able to recall information in a text. In fact, on the scale of comprehension, knowledge of the content is right at the bottom. When we discuss comprehension, here is what we mean.

Definition

> Ability to develop a justifiable, personal interpretation of a text.

Have you ever had this experience? You and a friend read the same news article about a new law that the government is trying to pass. You think the law is a terrible idea and that it shows how out of touch the government is. Your friend thinks the law would be a pretty good idea and that it shows the government understands how "common people" feel. You read the same article, but you have different reactions.

Perhaps you and a friend are reading the same book. The main character is going through a difficult time. You are bored by the book and think the main character is unrealistic. You think the story is predictable. Your friend is enthralled by the book and thinks the main character accurately represents what people actually experience during hardship. Your friend cannot wait to find out how the story ends. Again, you read the same text, but you have different reactions.

These are two very simplified examples, but there is a reason two people can read the same thing and have different impressions. When you read a book, article, advertisement, manual, etc., you interpret the text based on your existing knowledge, your experiences, your perspectives and philosophical outlook, and your general mental alertness and emotional state. When you are reading, you bring your whole self to the process.

Whether you are reading fiction or non-fiction, you will interpret the text. You will respond to the ideas and content, you will form an impression of the author, you will compare it to what you already know, and you will judge the value of the text as a whole. Your interpretation, your impression, of the text will, ultimately, be a combination of the words you read and your schema.

The concept of schema is critical to comprehension. In psychology, a schema is the way you perceive the world. Your schema is a merger of your perspectives, beliefs, experiences, and knowledge. It is the way you see the world and respond to new information and experiences. When you read something, you filter it through your schema to arrive at an interpretation. This is why two people can read the same thing and have two different reactions to it: they each have their own schema.

The concept of schema also relates to a concept that I mentioned in Chapter Two, "The Principles of Reading Instruction." In that chapter, I discussed how you learn new things based on what you already know. What you already know is part of your schema.

The Goal of Comprehension Instruction

The purpose of comprehension instruction is to help students make a justifiable, personal interpretation of a text. The interpretation will be based on the information in the text according to the student's schema. Let's look at the key words in this definition.

> *Justifiable:* demonstrate knowledge of the content and make a reasonable, logical conclusion about the information in the text
>
> *Personal:* based on the student's (not the teacher's) schema

In practical terms, you ask the student, "What does this mean to you and why?" In this process, you do two things.

First, you help the student understand the words, information, and concepts in the text. You help the student learn what the words mean, as well as the who, what, when, where, why, and how of the information in the text. Too often, comprehension instruction stops here. Once a student demonstrates knowledge of the content, the teacher moves on. This is very low level understanding, but there is more!

Second, you help the student determine the quality, value, usefulness, and application of the information. Even young children can do this. For example, with young readers, you might ask the following questions:

- Why do you think the character did...? (fiction)

- Have you heard any other stories like this? (fiction)

- Did you like it? Why? (fiction and nonfiction)
- Would you like to try something like this? Why? (fiction and nonfiction)
- Do you think this is true? Why? (nonfiction)
- Do you want to know more about this person or information? Why? (fiction and nonfiction)
- What would you do in this situation? Why? (fiction and nonfiction)

The basic approach to helping students comprehend a text is to ask the students what the text means to them and then to ask them why. Of course, you want to make sure students understand the words and information. These are steps towards comprehension. You want them to make sense of what they read. Once students get to that point, however, the focus of comprehension instruction shifts to evaluating and analyzing the information, combining or synthesizing the information with information from other text or experiences, and deciding what to do with the information.

And then you ask them, "Why?"

As it turns out, "why" is a powerful word. To answer that question, a student has to

- understand the content,
- think critically about the information,
- consider how the information relates to what he or she already knows,
- make logical conclusions, and
- communicate his or her ideas convincingly.

If a student can do this, you can conclude that the student comprehends the text. The goal of comprehension instruction is to make sure students can answer, and justify their answer to, "Why?"

Breaking Down Comprehension Skills

Reading comprehension has four sub-skills, three that lead to comprehension and one that occurs throughout the reading process. They are as follows.

Understanding: knowing the content

Making sense: considering the content and message

Applying: deciding what to do with, and using, the information

Self-monitoring: reflecting on whether or not you understand what you are reading

When we say that a student comprehends a text, we mean that the student can do the first three sub-skills. These sub-skills are not separate, and all three are required for comprehension.

Not only are these three skills necessary for comprehension but also they are used in order. First, a student needs to know and understand the content. The student needs to understand what the words mean and what information they communicate. Second, a student needs to reflect on and interpret the content. But there is one more step: applying. Once the student understands the content and has analyzed it, the final step is to determine what to do with the information.

The fourth sub-skill, self-monitoring, is what strong readers do while they are using the first three sub-skills. It is how students know they are doing the first three.

Explaining These Sub-skills

Understanding: In the context of reading comprehension, "understanding" means knowing what information the text is communicating. The first stage of understanding is knowing what the words mean. The second stage is putting those words together to understand the information. Understanding is about the facts being presented, the information about who, what, when, where, why, and how. Understanding, alone, is not comprehension. Instead, understanding is the first necessary step towards comprehension.

Making sense: With the sub-skill of making sense, students think critically about the information. This is the sub-skill where the concept of schema is so important. Making sense of the information requires the student to interpret the text. In fact, based on the discussion above, a student cannot help but to interpret the information.

When I discuss Bloom's Taxonomy and Depth of Knowledge a bit later, you will see that making sense is most of what students do once they understand the content. Making sense is the "heavy lifting" in comprehension because it requires the most mental work. In the meantime, here is a partial list of the types of activities students engage in when they are making sense:

> categorizing, comparing and contrasting, concluding, critiquing, discriminating, evaluating, generalizing, interpreting, modifying, organizing, predicting, proving, recommending, supporting, synthesizing, testing, verifying

Also, in the section below on discussion, which is the most effective strategy for comprehension instruction, you will see that discussion provides the training, opportunity, and support for making sense.

Applying: After figuring out what information is in the text (understanding) and interpreting the text (making sense), the student has to determine what to do with the information. This stage can seem tricky because it contains so many possibilities. Depending on the age and reading level of the student, the student may apply his or her understanding in the following ways:

- Decide to learn more about a topic, read more within the genre, or select other texts from an author;

- Participate in a discussion;

- Solve a problem or make a justifiable decision;

- Present the results of the analysis (through a speech, essay, picture, graphic, etc.) and try to convince other people that the student's interpretation is correct;

- Follow the steps, advice, or perspective presented by the author;

- Create new ideas or change current ideas based on the information;

- Write something that demonstrates support, disagrees, or presents alternatives; or

- Conduct a demonstration.

This is a very small sample set of possible applications, but it demonstrates that students have many options for applying what they read.

Application has one more purpose: assessment. When students can apply the information in a text, they demonstrate that they understand the content and have reflected, analyzed, and interpreted it. When students apply the information, you can assess their comprehension.

You can assess their understanding of the content, which is the first sub-skill, but you can only assess their comprehension when they use the sub-skill of application.

Self-monitoring: Self-monitoring is the most important sub-skill. As you read, or as a student reads, self-monitoring helps you decide whether or not you understand what you are reading. Strong readers do this continuously. Even while they are reading, they are assessing their level of understanding. They are always thinking about and questioning their understanding, always asking themselves, "Do I understand this?"

If they answer "yes," they continue reading. If they answer "no," they determine why they do not understand and seek to improve their understanding. Perhaps they do not understand the words, in which case they use various vocabulary skills to learn what the words mean. Perhaps they have missed some important information, in which case they re-read prior sections of the text. Perhaps they do not understand the concepts, in which case they may do a little research or review what they know and how it relates to the new information.

Good readers stop reading when they do not understand, and they do something to correct their lack of understanding. Because they are monitoring their understanding, strong readers are more likely to comprehend the text.

Weak readers, on the other hand, just keep reading. When they finish reading, they are left wondering what it was about.

Self-monitoring is a learned behavior. Although some students learn to do this naturally, many students need encouragement and activities that require them to stop reading and to gauge their understanding. Some students may believe that they will be punished or ridiculed if they admit to not understanding, so they keep silent. Others may have learned the mistaken idea that the point of reading is to get to the end, so they do not bother stopping to confirm their understanding. In most cases, however, weak readers simply never developed the habit of questioning their understanding.

Students can develop this habit if instructional activities require self-monitoring and if you model, encourage, and reward self-monitoring. It is the single most important difference between strong and weak readers.

Principles for Comprehension Instruction

Comprehension seems like a big, vague concept because it depends so heavily on personal interpretation of text. There might not be a single correct answer to the question "What does it mean?" Rather, students, like all readers, may have differing responses, interpretations, and reactions to the text they read. If they can show with logic, experience, and evidence that their interpretation is plausible, if they can demonstrate that information in the text supports their interpretation, they comprehend the text.

The instructional strategies and corresponding activities discussed later will describe how you can help students develop a personal, justifiable interpretation, which is the definition of comprehension. They are guided by four overarching principles for comprehension instruction.

1. Instruction needs to build background knowledge.

2. Instruction needs to require student work.

3. Instruction needs to facilitate collaboration.

4. Instruction needs to support differing opinions.

Build Background Knowledge

Whether students are reading fiction or non-fiction, they will need to know something about the topic. For example, they will likely need at least the following.

Nonfiction: basic information about the theme, issue, or topic; awareness of related concepts; historical information about the concepts; experience with the subject of the text; knowledge of basic vocabulary related to the subject. Without prior knowledge, readers cannot grasp the ideas and concepts being described and cannot determine either the quality of the information or how the information can be used.

Fiction: exposure to the genre; experiences, environment, or conditions similar to the character's; knowledge of the historical period (if relevant); understanding of the context or situation in which the events occur. Without prior knowledge, readers cannot understand the events described in the text and cannot form impressions of why they happen.

The first stage in comprehension instruction is to make sure students have the prior knowledge they need. Until that happens, students are not ready to comprehend the text. You want to know what students already know, and then you help them address any gaps in knowledge. You can help students build their background knowledge before they read the text, but I do not recommend it. New background knowledge is only relevant while students are reading the text. It does not have a purpose until students encounter information that requires it.

A better approach is to gauge students' understanding throughout the reading process and then help them build the background knowledge they need when they experience comprehension problems. Rather than waiting until students finish reading the entire text or designated portion (such as a chapter), provide multiple opportunities to stop reading, discuss what they understand or not, ask questions about the content, and gain the knowledge that will help them interpret what they are reading.

The only exception is vocabulary. Before beginning to read a new text, take time to identify and study unfamiliar words. See the chapter on vocabulary for information and strategies for studying vocabulary prior to reading.

Require Student Work

The best advice I ever received during teacher training was in the form of a question: What do you want students to do? More than 30 years later, I still consider this question every time I provide training and professional development for adults. This question is particularly important to comprehension instruction.

Because we are helping students develop their own justifiable interpretation, they need to do most of the work. The work can take many forms, some of which you will see later in the sample activities. It includes graphic organizers, reflective writing, research, and discussion. Overall, we want students to think critically about the text, consider how the content aligns with their schema, engage in analysis and further study, and determine how they can use the information. We can not do this for them: they have to do the work themselves.

Facilitate Collaboration

As mentioned in chapter two, "Principles of Reading Instruction," students learn to read by working together. This is especially important for comprehension. The more perspectives, experiences, ideas, and information a student has available when reading a text, the more able the student will be to create a justifiable interpretation. Of course, students bring their own schema to the process, but they can also draw from the schema of other students. For this to happen, students need to collaborate on comprehension activities.

Your role, then, is to design instructional activities that student can work on together. There is a place for individual work, but students will benefit from combining their individual efforts into a collaborative effort. They can compare their ideas, share information and perspectives, and constructively criticize their own and other students' ideas. For example, you might have students create their own graphic organizers, which they can then discuss with other students to create a graphic organizer that encompasses their mutual ideas.

The next section, "What Works for Comprehension Instruction," will address the strategy of discussion. Discussion is the most powerful strategy for improving reading comprehension. The main reason why it is so powerful is discussion allows for sharing ideas and information to help all participating students deepen and strengthen their comprehension of the text and develop a personal, justifiable interpretation. Students cannot have discussions alone. They must do it together.

Support Differing Opinions

The goal of comprehension instruction is not for all students to agree, whether with each other or with you. The goal is to help students develop an interpretation that they can justify. When student work collaboratively, when they are asking questions and providing ideas, when they are adding to their knowledge and to each other's, when they are providing their interpretations receiving feedback, they will develop and adjust their interpretations until they are able to justify them.

This process will have one of two outcomes. Either students will develop a shared interpretation or they will develop differing interpretations. If, following discussion, students have differing interpretations of the text, then the result looks like this:

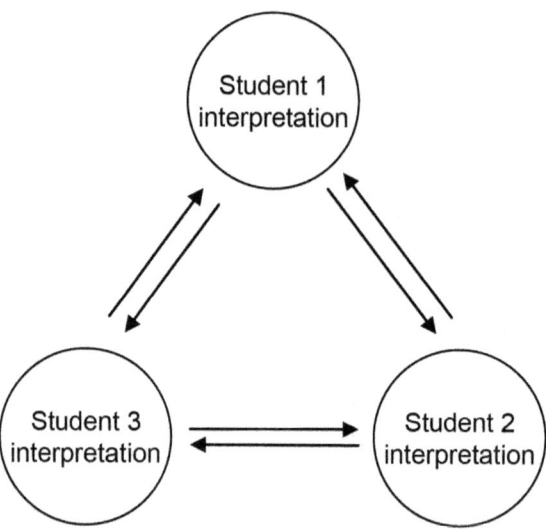

As depicted here, students are sharing information and ideas with one another, but they still apply their individual schema to create different interpretations.

On the other hand, if they find a common interpretation, then the result looks like this:

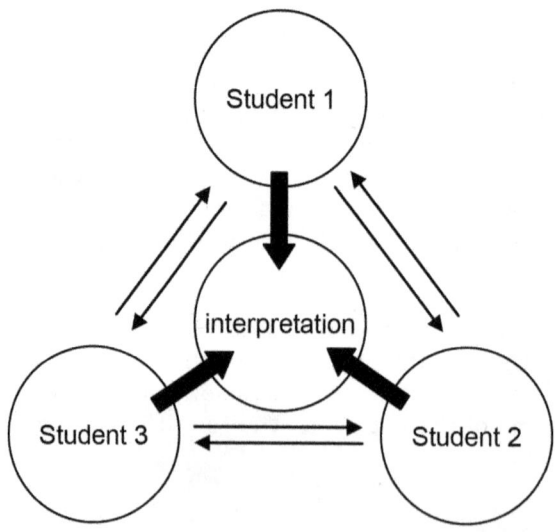

As depicted in this image, students are sharing information and ideas with one another, but they create a common interpretation of the text. Very often, students will begin with their individual interpretations and then, through collaboration, modify or enhance their understandings to reach a shared conclusion about the text.

Both are acceptable, and both outcomes should be encouraged. In fact, differing opinions provide great opportunities for critical analysis. Students can compare and contrast their ideas, identify strengths and weaknesses of others' ideas, and learn to argue constructively to support their own ideas. And that leads to comprehension.

What Works for Comprehension Instruction

If you could do only one thing to help students develop comprehension, I would say read with students and talk about what you read. Although that would be an exceptional beginning, it would not be enough, nor is it the only strategy for helping students develop their comprehension. And, quite frankly, it would be rather boring to do only that.

When we consider the definition of comprehension and the instructional principles for comprehension, we see that a variety of strategies will be effective.

Six Sample Strategies for Comprehension Instruction

- Discussion
- Graphic organizers
- Retelling & summarizing
- Writing
- Pre-questioning and prediction
- Comprehension self-monitoring

Discussion: Discussion is the number one strategy for helping students improve their comprehension, and I will address it in much greater detail later.

In brief, discussion is the opportunity to share ideas and information, listen to others' ideas, support or oppose those ideas with reasons, and ask and answer questions. Participating meaningfully and constructively in a discussion requires a student (or anyone!) to maintain a respectful attitude, to focus on the topic and not the person, and to demonstrate no small amount of humility.

The two most important things to remember about discussion are as follows.

1. Students should be encouraged to discuss with each other, as opposed to simply answering the your questions. Your questions may lead to discussion among students, but answering questions without follow-up discussion is assessment, not instruction.

2. Questions, both the yours and the students', need to address the multiple levels of Bloom's Taxonomy or Depth of Knowledge. The who, what, when, where, why, and how types of questions are the lowest level of discussion, not only because they focus on recall rather than comprehension but also because they lead to right vs. wrong answers and not interpretation. (More about this later.)

Graphic Organizers: When you read, your brain makes categories of details and facts, mental links between various disparate bits of information, groups of similar types of information, pathways representing order and sequence, and connections between words and approximate meanings. This is how your brain makes sense of so many details and so much information. This is what brains do, and they are typically very good at it. But they need help. How should the information be connected? What is the similar information? How should information be sequenced? And so on.

We can use graphic organizers to help our brains collect, sort, categorize, and connect information in a useful manner. The basic principle is this: we organize the information graphically to learn how to do it mentally. This is brain training. Obviously, as we become adult readers with strong reading skills, we do not need to do this, although many people may take notes or make outlines while reading. (I do this sometimes if I am having difficulty understanding technical or highly conceptual information.)

The other value of graphic organizers is that they serve as communication tools for sharing one's ideas with other people. You can use them to present information (for example, graphs) and to focus and organize your thoughts as you speak about a topic (for example, flow charts).

Graphic organizers come in many different forms. A quick Internet search will provide you with many samples. As you consider which types of graphic organizers you want students to create or complete, first consider what purpose they will serve and what you want students to learn. Once you determine the learning objective, then select the type that will be most useful. Do not select graphic organizers because they are pretty or fun. Select them because they are appropriate for the learning objective.

Sample Learning Purposes	Example Graphic Organizers
sequence of events	plot line
relationships between people	bubble chart
order of steps and options	flow chart
relationship between ideas	concept map
compare and contrast opinions or perspectives	Venn diagram

Students can create or complete the graphic organizers on their own or together. If they work on them alone, then they should do one of two things as a next step:

1. compare them with other students' graphic organizers and, through discussion, create a common graphic organizer on which they can agree, or
2. share them in small-group discussion to help present their ideas and to understand other students' ideas.

The one thing they should not be asked to do is to turn them in for grading. You might be able to give a grade for completion, but it has no value for helping students strengthen their ideas or improve their comprehension.

Retelling and summarizing: You may have heard the adage that the best way to learn something is to teach it. Retelling and summarizing are two ways that we apply this adage to comprehension instruction. These two skills are related, but they are different.

Retelling focuses on content information. When students retell text, they have to recall key facts and ideas, and they have to put them in sequence. They also have to distinguish between important and non-important information. (For example, retelling the story of Homer's *Ulysses* would include important events that took place at each island he visited on the way back to Greece.)

Summarizing focuses on concepts. When students summarize

text, they have to think about the themes, purposes, intentions, categories of information, as well as key information that demonstrates those concepts. They also have to group information into broad categories that encompass a collection of facts and information. (For example, a summary of Homer's *Ulysses* would discuss that Ulysses visited multiple islands on the way home to Greece and ran into serious trouble at each one that only he could solve through bravery, cunning, and luck.)

Retelling is a challenging skill, but summarizing is even more difficult. For younger students, learning to retell the content may be sufficient. A common retelling task for students is to have them relate the story, information, or key information in a certain number of words, 50 to 200 or so. As students get older, however, and can start exploring themes and concepts, they should begin working on summarization skills.

Design activities that require one or both of these skill sets, such as writing or discussion. Students may need to reflect on the text first, such as through using a graphic organizer. Additionally, to assist in this process, consider asking specific questions about the text and have students include their answers in their retelling or summary.

Most importantly, retelling and summarizing require an audience, whether one person or many. After students retell or summarize, they should participate in follow-up discussion with other students, perhaps with some specific questions from you to help guide the discussion.

Writing: When students write about what they have read, they have to recall and reflect on the information, and they have to figure how to communicate their ideas clearly. These are all important steps for developing comprehension.

You can approach this instructional strategy from many different perspectives, such as asking students to write their impressions in reading journals, to respond to open-ended questions, or to develop a theme and write about it. Younger students can do this, too. For example, you can ask them to draw the scene that they think is most interesting and then explain why they choose it. The point of writing as an instructional strategy is for students to reflect on—and communicate about—on the text.

Writing can be a solitary task, which makes it incomplete as a strategy for developing comprehension. After students write, they need to share or present their ideas to other students for discussion, feedback, and constructive criticism. I would also recommend that before students write, they also engage in collaborative work, such as developing a graphic organizer of ideas to include in their writing piece. Ultimately, writing as an instructional method, needs to be embedded in a broader, collaborative set of activities.

Pre-questioning and prediction: "What do you want to know? What do you think is next?" These are two powerful questions to ask students as you help them develop their comprehension skills. To answer either of these questions, students have to think critically about what they already know, whether about the author, the information, or the characters. They have to look for patterns in the text and make an evaluation of the author.

The follow-up instructional activities are based on similar questions. "Were your questions answered?" "Did you learn what you expected?" "How accurate were your predictions?"

Answering these questions is sophisticated, but students of all ages can do it. The most important benefit of asking these questions is to help students to develop the habit of asking them when reading alone.

Comprehension self-monitoring: Of all the skills students need to improve their comprehension, self-monitoring is the most important. I discussed self-monitoring in the section on comprehension sub-skills, so why is it also here under strategies?

For every instructional activity in which students are reading, you want to include specific points for students to stop reading and assess whether or not they understand what they are reading. Students need to develop the habit of questioning their own understanding, which means you have to keep providing opportunities for students to ask, "Do I understand what I am reading?"

Often, the first time a teacher gauges a student's level of comprehension is during some form of application or assessment. This is too late. If asked, most students can state whether or not they are understanding the text. The problem is that students might not stop to consider their understanding, and they forge right ahead to get to the end. You need to help them ask the question for themselves.

There are many ways to do this. Of course, if students are reading aloud, you simply stop them and ask, "What do you think that means? What do you know about [blank]?" You also need to include opportunities to monitor their understanding during other types of comprehension activities. For example, when students are creating graphic organizers, they can leave blanks for unknown information, include questions they want answered, or create a T-chart of information they understand and do not understand. If students are retelling or summarizing, orally or in writing, you can have them include a list of "things I don't understand."

As you can see, comprehension self-monitoring is not a strategy that you use by itself. It is a strategy that you embed throughout the other strategies.

Sample Activities for Comprehension

Most of the comprehension lessons you plan will incorporate more than one strategy (and they should all include comprehension self-monitoring and discussion). For example, if you have a writing activity, you may have students "pre-write" by collaboratively developing a graphic organizer, and you may follow the writing activity with discussion or a follow-up written piece in which students discuss how their ideas compare with other students' ideas.

The sample activities below generally correspond to a single strategy, but a well-designed lesson will have students perform several activities to address multiple strategies.

Strategy	Sample Activity Types	Comprehension Sub-skills
Discussion	Creating questions	All sub-skills
	Group brainstorming and decision making (e.g., nominal group technique)	
	Structured debate	
	Discussion board / forum	
	Read-respond-share	

Graphic Organizers	Plot lines	Understanding
	Timelines	Making sense
	Semantic maps	
	Venn diagrams	
	T-charts for comparison	
	Cause and effect charts	
Retelling & Summarizing	Gallery / book walks	Understanding
	Book/story review	Making sense
	Group-generated choral read	
	Snowball discussion	
Writing	Reflection journal	Making sense
	Comic strip	Applying
	Book/story review	Self-monitoring
	Response to higher-level question	
	Promotional posters	
	Discussion board / forum	
	Sticky notes	

Pre-questioning and Prediction	KWL chart (know, want to know, learned)	Understanding
		Self-monitoring
	T-chart for questions and answers	
	Posing research questions to other student groups	
	Completing stories	
Comprehension Self-monitoring	Thumbs up / thumbs down	Self-monitoring
		Understanding
	KWL chart	Making sense
	Research questions	
	T-charts	
	Paraphrasing	

The Number One Strategy: Discussion

Remember, the definition of comprehension is the ability to develop a justifiable, personal interpretation of text. It is the ability to say, "Here is what this means to me, and this is the reason why." You can approach comprehension instruction in many ways (and you should), but one way is better than all others: discussion.

In chapter four, I discussed how discussion helps students develop their oral language skills, and I described discussion like this: Discussion is not about responding to questions with the "right" answer. Discussion is

- sharing one's own ideas,
- asking questions,
- agreeing and disagreeing,
- explaining and defending a position,
- contributing more information, and

- expanding on others' ideas.

When students are discussing a text, not only do they refine their own ideas but also they help other student's refine theirs.

Discussion is more than sitting around and talking at random. As the teacher, your primary role during discussion is to ask questions that help students reflect on the content, their own ideas, and the information and ideas that other students share. To a lesser degree, your role is also to (a) provide additional background information and (b) encourage students to consider specific content within the text that might help them modify their interpretations.

To lead a productive discussion, you need a good plan and the right approach. The plan is the purpose you want students to accomplish and the questions you will ask to help them achieve that purpose. The approach is the way you interact with the students and get them to interact with each other. Stay away from the yes/no and true/false questions, and refrain from suggesting that students are right or wrong. Instead, ask them to justify their ideas and to respond to other students' ideas, provide additional information and ask them how it relates to their ideas, and get them talking to one another!

Before engaging students in discussion, consider the questions that you are going to ask. Certainly, you will want to ask questions to make sure they know the facts in the content, such as the who, what, when, where, and how information. Once you are past those questions, though, you will want to ask "higher order questions" that require deeper thinking and reflection about the text. Bloom's Taxonomy and Depth of Knowledge provide excellent guidance for these questions. They also give you clues about what students can do to demonstrate thinking at that level.

Bloom's Taxonomy and Discussion

By definition, "taxonomy" means a system for categorizing and classifying information. Bloom's Taxonomy (revised 2001) is one way to categorize various types of thinking skills and processes. For many years, until Depth of Knowledge gained popularity, I would point to Bloom's Taxonomy and recommend that teachers use it to plan for discussion. (I still do!) From the lowest-level thinking skills (#1) to the highest-level thinking skills (#6), Bloom's taxonomy is as follows.

Level	Central Question	Possible Actions
1. Remembering	What is the information?	define
		describe
		label
		list
2. Understanding	What messages or ideas does the text present?	restate
		paraphrase
		summarize
		defend
		extend
3. Applying	What can you do with the information?	organize
		choose
		produce
		solve
		decide
4. Analyzing	How does the information compare with other information?	categorize
		compare
		infer
		prioritize
5. Evaluating	What are the quality and value of the information?	judge
		critique
		consider
		recommend
		compare

| 6. Creating | How can you merge the information with information from other sources to create new knowledge? | compose hypothesize create combine predict |

Notice three things about this taxonomy.

1. Knowledge is the lowest level. Recalling information requires the least thinking. If you never get beyond the knowledge level, you cannot comprehend text.

2. To attain the definition of reading comprehension, students must apply all levels.

3. Students can do many things to demonstrate that they addressing each level of the taxonomy.

Also, notice one very important issue about the levels. Although students can perform these actions in many different ways, they can perform them all during discussion. This is one reason that discussion is so powerful for developing comprehension. As you are planning for the discussion, make sure to include questions that will require students to match each level of Bloom's Taxonomy.

Can young children conduct such sophisticated thinking skills? Absolutely. Perhaps the depth and complexity of thinking will be low-level, but the thinking process can be high level. Let's say you just read two short books to a group of four-year-old children. Ask them to pick their favorite book and tell you why they liked it better. That is evaluation, the highest level of thinking skills on Bloom's Taxonomy.

Depth of Knowledge and Discussion

Depth of Knowledge is increasingly popular in education circles, and many teachers I have worked with are expected to use it by their school administrators. Dr. Norman Webb's Depth of Knowledge taxonomy helps educators develop assessments that measure different ways for students to demonstrate understanding.

The purposes of Depth of Knowledge in reading are (1) to describe how deeply students must understand the content and (2) to describe how in-depth students will share their knowledge.

How extensively will students be asked to demonstrate their understanding? For example, does an assessment (or lesson objective) require students to recall the facts or to use their knowledge to create something new? The four levels of Depth of Knowledge (for reading) describe how deeply students must understand what they read and how extensively they use what they understand. The questions you ask during discussion determine what the students do with their knowledge and how they use their knowledge to respond.

The four Depth of Knowledge levels are as follows.

Level	Central Questions	Possible Actions*
DOK-1: Recall and Reproduce Knowledge	What knowledge has the student acquired?	recall answer quote list
DOK-2: Apply Knowledge	How can the knowledge be used?	interpret estimate classify predict
DOK-3: Analyze Knowledge	Why is the knowledge valuable, relevant, and useful?	revise assess compare conclude
DOK-4: Transfer and Extend Knowledge	How else can the knowledge be used?	synthesize connect design create

*Note: These actions represent various manners of demonstrating knowledge, not the complexity of mental actions or processes.

Notice two things about this taxonomy.

1. Each level assumes that the student already has knowledge and understanding of the text.
2. Each level has many actions for students to demonstrate knowledge at that level, and each action can be conducted in many different ways.

Bloom's Taxonomy or Depth of Knowledge?

When I provide professional development on reading, I discuss using Bloom's Taxonomy as a guide for planning discussion. Teachers can use Bloom's Taxonomy to pose discussion questions that require higher-order thinking skills and that lead to comprehension. I am regularly asked about using Depth of Knowledge instead of Bloom's Taxonomy. The answer, unfortunately, is "depends."

Bloom's Taxonomy and Depth of Knowledge have different purposes.

Bloom's Taxonomy	**Depth of Knowledge**
various levels of thinking skills	various ways of demonstrating knowledge
least to highest-order thinking skills	simplest to most extensive way to demonstrate knowledge
used to increase cognitive rigor	used to increase expression of knowledge

A common misconception about Depth of Knowledge is that higher levels actions require more sophisticated mental processes. They do not...at least not inherently. The level of thinking does not depend on the action but on what students are asked to do with the action. Level one is pretty straightforward, and requires the least mental processing, but after that, things get muddy.

The level of thinking required to perform some actions in level two may be more complex than performing some actions in level four. For example, a student may be able to connect (level four) knowledge about horses to a story about a character who rides horses, but might not be able to predict (level two) what will happen next in the story.

The so-called DOK wheel promotes this misconception by placing action verbs in various quadrants of the wheel. ("So-called" because Dr. Webb did not create it and has noted that it does not accurately reflect the principles and purpose of the Depth of Knowledge taxonomy.) Teachers might assume that if they have students perform certain actions, they are asking students to use different levels of thinking. In reality, the level of thinking depends on what cognitive processes are required to conduct those actions for that specific lesson. For example, level three includes the verb "compare," but what are students comparing? Comparing the way two characters talk is not too challenging, but comparing the writing of two journalists to determine bias about a topic is quite challenging.

So the answer is "depends." If you are helping students develop the higher-order thinking skills for comprehension, use Bloom's Taxonomy. If you are helping students demonstrate their knowledge to different degrees, use Depth of Knowledge. Both taxonomies are useful as you engage students in discussion or other instructional activities for comprehension. Using either system will help students achieve the expectations of the other system.

If you use Bloom's Taxonomy to plan for discussion:

> prepare questions based on a variety of levels, aiming towards the top level. Start by assessing basic knowledge (level one), then advance upwards towards level six.

If you use Depth of Knowledge to plan for discussion:

> prepare questions that ask students to perform a variety of actions for each level, but sequence them from "easier" to "harder" questions. Start by assessing basic knowledge (level one), and then ask questions that reflect the other three levels, using your best guess to estimate which questions will be more difficult to answer.

What Does Not Work for Comprehension Instruction

Regardless of the strategies and activities you use, keep in mind the goal of comprehension instruction and make sure that what students do helps them achieve that goal. Not everything will. Listed below are some common strategies that do not help students develop a justifiable, personal interpretation of text.

Strategy	Reason Why It Does Not Work
Quizzes (computer based or otherwise)	Quizzes are assessment, not instruction. They address the lowest level of knowledge and thinking, recall, because that is the only thing they can assess easily. They cannot address higher levels of thinking or other forms of demonstration, and they do not include opportunities to explore ideas, refine justifications, or build background knowledge. To the extent they attempt to address higher levels, they still assume a single correct interpretation, regardless of the student's personal and justifiable interpretation. In brief, they do not and cannot measure comprehension.
Individual Instruction	I would call this minimally effective. A teacher and student can work together, can have discussions, and can perform a variety of tasks to demonstrate knowledge—all of which lead to comprehension. On the other hand, without other students or other people involved, the instructional value will be limited.
True/False, Yes/No, and Right/Wrong Questions	The point of comprehension instruction is not to get the right answer but to develop a defensible interpretation. Questions that only allow a "correct" answer do not lead to this goal.
Sustained Silent Reading (SSR)	SSR is not comprehension instruction. It might be a precursor to instruction, and it might be used as a first step towards developing comprehension, but it is not instruction by itself. This is not to say that students should not read to themselves, but this is not enough.

Arts and Crafts	Draw me a picture of.... Create a model of.... Etc. Although fun and engaging, these are not instruction. They might be used as assessment if students are required to apply their knowledge in some way or use them to respond to a higher-order question. You could also use them to increase students' interest in a text.
Round Robin Reading	With round robin reading, students take turns reading aloud. Round robin reading does not address any levels of Bloom's Taxomony and generally does little to improve students' knowledge of the content.

Companion Reading Components

Comprehension draws from several other reading components: phonics, vocabulary, and oral language. If you are focusing on helping students improve their comprehension skills, you will also need to provide instructional activities in phonics, vocabulary, and oral language at the same time. The activities for those components should apply to the text you want students to comprehend.

Phonics: Phonics leads to understanding the words in text, which means it leads to understanding the content of a text. This is part of the first step towards comprehension.

Vocabulary: Students have to know what the words mean, not just the dictionary definitions but how they are being used by the author or characters. By studying the vocabulary, students will have a better understanding of the content, which they will need to form an interpretation of the text. Here, the study of vocabulary overlaps with the study of oral language.

Oral Language: How we interpret a text depends, in great part, on whether we understand what the author or characters mean by the words they use. We interpret the way language is used to form an interpretation of the text. Any study of how language is being used will help students form an impression or interpretation.

Chapter 10
The Love of Reading

As a teacher of reading (whether you are a classroom teacher, homeschool parent, or reading interventionist), your job is to help students learn to read well. That is your entire job, and that is the point of this book. I sometimes make the controversial statement that it does not matter whether or not students enjoy reading. The only thing that matters is whether or not they can do it well.

From an instructional, academic perspective, this is true. Students are not graded on their enjoyment of reading. They do not pass or fail their classes because they love reading. If they are required to read something as part of their job or their school work, if they need to read something to solve a problem or determine a solution, enjoyment is irrelevant. Can they do it or not?

But this perspective seems very shallow to me. Shouldn't students also love reading, or at least enjoy it?

Three Types of Love of Reading

What is the "love of reading"? When people talk about loving reading, they are likely referring to one of three things.

1. Love of the content.

    The content means the subject matter and how it is presented.

    Some people love reading about history because they are interested in history topics. Other people may love reading science fiction novels because they are interested in how stories occur in those contexts. Yet others love reading novels because they are interested in the experiences of other people. Some people love reading texts by certain authors because they trust that those authors will present new or different perspectives and different ways of considering topics. I have friends who love reading medical and scientific research journals because they are interested in new approaches and ideas about health and medicine.

    Thus, some people love reading because they have a positive emotional or cognitive reaction to the content of the texts they read.

2. Love of the process of reading.

The process of reading means the behaviors of reading and the environment in which reading occurs.

Some people love reading because they value the relaxation they experience when they read. Other people love reading because it distracts them from other difficulties they may be experiencing. Yet other people love reading because of the sense of satisfaction and fulfillment they experience when they finish with a text. Many people love reading because they associate it with other enjoyable experiences, such as sitting in an easy chair while drinking coffee.

Thus, some people love reading because they have positive emotional or cognitive reaction to the behaviors they engage in while reading, the effect of reading on their emotional or mental state, and environment in which they read.

3. Love of the text.

The text is the words found in the text and how the author puts them together to make meaning.

Some people love reading poetry because they find the word choices, rhythms, and order aesthetically pleasing. Some people love reading particular authors because those authors use specific agreeable styles and approaches to presenting their ideas. Yet other people love reading because they like the sounds of words, the way grammar and meaning interact, and how a word choice or order affects the interpretation.

Thus, some people love reading because they have a positive emotional or cognitive reaction to the way words affect their interpretation and interaction with text.

Helping Students Love Reading

When you consider encouraging students to love reading, or at least enjoy it, you have to keep two principles in mind.

1. You cannot make students love reading. Your enjoyment of reading may increase the likelihood that they will enjoy reading because they see that enjoyment is possible. But

you cannot make them love it. You can neither require nor expect that students will have the same reaction to reading that you have.

2. The reason why you love reading is personal to you. The reason you may have for loving reading may not align with the students' interests, needs, or personalities. The same things that bring you pleasure when reading might have no appeal to students. You are not them, and they are not you.

On the other hand, you can **increase the potential for students to love reading**.

The most important thing you can do is teach students to read well. If students do not learn to read well, they will never find it enjoyable. Reading will always be an unpleasant chore. Help them learn to read, and help them find texts that are appropriate for their developing reading ability.

The second most important thing you can do is to help them identify and acquire texts that align with their interests. If they are not interested in what they are reading, they will have little reason to do it. "Love of the content" is only one type of loving reading, but nothing else will matter if they are disinterested or bored by the content. Conversely, if they have texts that are interesting, then they will have a reason to learn to read, and they will have interest in reading more.

The third most important thing you can do is to demonstrate your own enthusiasm for reading. Students need to see that reading can be enjoyable and satisfying. They need role models, people they respect or admire, who engage in reading. Your enthusiasm for reading can provoke their interest in reading, too.

Will these actions make students love reading? Not necessarily, though they will increase the chance that students will learn to love reading. Even if they never "love" reading, they will learn that reading—and learning to read—is valuable.

And for many students, that will be enough.

Thank you for helping children learn to read.

Appendix A
Description of the Sample Activities

The following activities and brief descriptions are sample activities to address the various reading components.

These activities may or may not work for your students. Consider whether or not they will be useful to you, how you might modify them for your students, and what other ideas they might suggest.

Oral Language Development Activities

Activity	Description
Cause and effect study	A study of the words someone used and the reaction by the person who hears them.
	Students consider how a character speaks or the author writes, and determines the effects, positive or negative. This can be done by a T-chart, graphic organizer, or discussion. Also, a study of other ways something might be said and how the reaction might be different.
Character analysis	Students study how a particular character speaks, including the word choices, phrasing, tone, etc., and what the manner of speaking indicates about the character.
Choral reading	Small or large group of students read aloud together multiple times, with in-between discussion of the phrasing, emphasis, or tone of voice.

Close-reading	Students conduct an in-depth examination of particular word choices and the intended and received messages that those choices communicate.
Discussion	Small groups discuss responses to questions about language use, word choices, cause and effect, and multiple ways to communicate the same idea.
Explicit instruction	The teacher directly teaches particular word choices, sentences, and ways to communicate various ideas; teaches specific language patterns for the students to use, such as how to ask a question or respectfully indicate disagreement.
Graphic organizers followed by discussion	Individual students or small groups work on a graphic organizer about words, such as multiple words with similar meanings, effect of language choices, connotative meanings of words, or character analysis of speech and word patterns. This is a good preliminary step for meaningful interaction in a discussion to share similar or different interpretations.
Guided oral reading	A highly recommended strategy. One student reads aloud, and the teacher or another student listens. The student receives feedback on phrasing, expression, and emphasis, and then reads the same passage aloud. This can occur with multiple repetitions.
Reading and writing skits	After reading a skit together, students discuss the various characters, expressions, tone, etc., and then the students take roles in the skit to read aloud. The same skit should be read more than once, with discussion and feedback between each reading.

Revising and rewording	Students identify other ways to say the same thing, whether revising an expression entirely or simply changing words to produce a different effect.
Rhyming and "word play"	Students find as many rhymes as possible for a particular word. This can be in the form of a contest to see who can identify the most words. Another way is to use rhyming poetry or songs and change the rhyming words to other rhyming words to change the meaning. This can get a bit silly, which is fun.
Short-answer questions	Students respond to the teacher's open-ended questions about word choices, language use, appropriate expressions for a particular situation, etc.
Student-created questions followed by discussion	Same as short-answer questions, but the students generate the questions. After the short answers are given, the teacher leads a discussion about differences in the answers, and students may keep or modify their responses.
Teaching language patterns	The teacher directly teaches particular word choices, sentences, and ways to communicate various ideas; teaches specific language patterns for the students to use, such as how to ask a question or respectfully indicate disagreement. Students practice the patterns and then use them in discussion or mock-situations.
Text analysis followed by discussion	Students analyze a character's or author's use of the language, with attention paid to the character's / author's style and whether or not the style supports the purpose.
Word groups	Students use a graphic organizer or create a list of words that have similar meanings or purposes.

Writing prompts followed by discussion	Similar to short-answer questions, but the students write their response before discussing them as a small group. The prompts may also be topics for reflection.

Phonemic Awareness Activities

Activity	Description
Alphabet song	Students sing any one of the variations of alphabet songs. As students sing the song, they indicate, hold up, point to, etc. the letter. (Example, students can have a chart of all the letters, and as they sing the "standard" alphabet song, they point to the letter.)
Call-and-response	The teacher asks students to perform some modification to the sounds of a word, such as changing the starting sound from one sound to another, and then saying the resulting word.
Clapping sounds / syllables	Students clap every time they hear a specific sound or for each syllable.
Creating rhymes	Students find as many rhymes as possible for a particular word. This can be in the form of a contest to see who can identify the most words. Another way is to use rhyming poetry or songs and change the rhyming words to other rhyming words, filling in the end of a line with a rhyming word, or making up an entirely new line in the poem that fits the rhyming pattern.
Exaggerated recitation	Students read aloud a poem or story by over-expressing the words (e.g., making the entire piece seem super exciting).

Explicit instruction	The teacher directly teaches the sounds or sound combinations within words and has students practice them.
Fill in missing words (based on a rhyme)	Similar to creating rhymes, students complete the line in a rhyming couplet or poem.
Finding rhymes	Small groups or individual students find rhyming words, through oral response, graphic organizer, or a list.
I-Spy	The teacher says, "I spy with my little eye something that has the sound...," followed by the target sound. Students find objects with a name that contain a target sound, whether the first, last, or middle sounds. There can be more than one right answer.
Letter bingo	Using bingo-type cards with words on them, students mark those words that have a given sound or number of syllables. (This combines phonics and phonemic awareness.)
Marking written poetry	Students circle, or otherwise mark, words that have particular sounds or sounds that are similar to a word spoken by the teacher. (This combines phonics and phonemic awareness.)
Matching pictures to words	Students identify pictures of things with specific sounds in a word spoken by the teacher.
Matching words by sounds	Students list or state words that have a specific sound.
Metered poetry	In small groups or as a class, students memorize and recite short poems.

Pair blending	The teacher or a student says the first part of a word, and the other student says the second part. This can be expanded to multiple parts for multiple students.
Pair response to questions	A version of call and response, students ask their partners to modify the sounds within a word. This may produce nonsense words, which is acceptable.
Short-answer questions	The teacher asks students to identify words that have given sounds in a particular location within the word. Each word students identify is sounded out.
Sing-along	Students memorize and sing short rhyming songs.
Sound boards	Students place markers along a picture of a ladder or row of boxes, one marker per sound within a word. Students compare their answers and try to sound out the word with as many sounds as they have identified. Then they blend the individual words together.
Sound picture charts	Students look at pictures of items and sound out their names, with the items having the same sound in their names.
Sound removal	Students sound out a word, and then, at the teacher's direction, remove one of the sounds to see what word results.
Sounding out words	Self-explanatory: students say the word, then say each sound in the word.
Teacher-led oral practice	There are several ways to do this: the teacher says and then sounds out words containing the same sound for students to echo or as a call-and-response.
Word grouping	Students identify and list a set of words that all contain the target sound.

Word grouping by sound counts	Students identify and list words that have the same number of sounds.
Word swapping	Students change words in rhyming poetry or song to fit the rhyme or to add words that have a specific sound.

Phonics Activities

Activity	Description
Call-and-response blending	The teacher holds up a card with letters to represent a sound; the student does the same. Together they speak the teacher's sound, then the student's. They say the resulting word together.
Choral reading	Small or large groups of students read aloud together multiple times, with in-between discussion of the decoding of the words that students mispronounced.
Finding rhymes / rhyming poetry	Students circle words within a poem that rhyme, and draw lines from one rhyming word to another.
Flash cards	The teacher prepares a stack of cards contains words with the letter–sound associations being studied. The teacher or another student holds up a card. Once it is read aloud correctly, the card is returned to the stack of words. Go through the entire stack several times for practice, even if the student decodes them correctly.
Graphic organizers	Using a variety of graphic organizers, such as bubble graphs, students break words into letter–sound combinations, include definitions and uses of the word, and similes and antonyms. (This exact exercise works for vocabulary, too.)

Guided oral reading	A highly recommended strategy. One student reads aloud, and the teacher or another student listens. The student receives feedback on decoding, and the teacher and student read aloud together. The student then reads the same passage aloud. This can occur with multiple repetitions.
Identifying site words in text	Self-explanatory: using the list of words containing the target letter–sound associations, students find the words in text. They should engage in guided oral reading of the passages.
I-Spy	The teacher calls out a letter or group of letters that make a specific sound, and students search for visible things with names that contain the sound.
Journaling	Writing in a personal journal, such as a reading journal. Students use specific words in their journal entry that contain various letter–sound association being studied.
Odd word out	Looking at a set of words, students identify the word that does not contain the letter–sound association being studied.
Quick erase / swap	The teacher writes a word, and the students decode it. The teacher removes or changes letters in the word to create a new word, which the student decode.
Rhyming poetry	Students write rhyming poems or couplets in which the rhyming words contain letter–sound association being studied.
Sound searching	Students search text to find words that have a specific sound(s).

Sound timelines	After sounding out words, students write out words with spaces or dashes between each sound in the word.
Syllabification	Students break written words into syllables, either orally or in writing.
Vocabulary study prior to reading	Students sound out (and study) the vocabulary terms and new words that they are going to find in the text they are about to read. (This should be a part of all vocabulary activities.)
Vocabulary substitution	When studying antonyms and synonyms, students sound out and practice decoding new words, which they then use as replacements during vocabulary activities.
Word analysis for roots	Identifying and sounding out root words that have the letter–sound association being studied.
Word grouping by letter combinations	Identifying or listing words that have the letter–sound association being studied.
Word searches in text	Similar to vocabulary study prior to reading and identifying sight words in text, students identify words in text that have the letter–sound association being studied.

Fluency Activities

Activity	Description
Choral reading with follow-up	Small or large group of students reading aloud together multiple times, with in-between discussion of the decoding, expression, and pacing.

Choral reading text summary	Students in small groups prepare a summary of the text they are reading and then perform a choral reading of their summary.
Close reading with guided oral reading	A highly recommended strategy. One student reads aloud, and the teacher or another student listens. The student receives feedback on decoding, expression, and pacing. Next, the teacher and student read aloud together. The student then reads the same passage aloud. This can occur with multiple repetitions.
Discussion on interpretation, followed by choral reading	Students discuss the tone and expression of a text, considering the author's or character's intention, and then practice and perform a choral reading with appropriate pace and expression.
Dramatic oral reading of a poem	Following discussion of pacing and expression, students read aloud a poem (or other text).
Partner reading with discussion	Similar to guided oral reading, but with another student providing feedback and practice. Following the oral readings, students discuss a set of questions generated by the teacher or other students.
Plays and skits	Students discuss the characters in a poem and consider how the text can be expressed and with what pacing that would be appropriate for the character's personality, intentions, and emotion. Then the students take roles in the skit to read aloud. The same skit should be read more than once, with discussion and feedback between each reading.

Randomized small-group choral reading	Students in pairs or small groups chorally read aloud a section of the text. The teacher (or other students) select the next pair to read aloud. This is similar to "round-robin" style reading, but students do not know which section they will be called upon to read and they will read aloud together. Student pairs should practice the entire selection first.
Recorded choral reading	Students record their choral reading, review the recording, discuss modifications, and then do it again.
Team echo reading with discussion	Pairs (or small groups) of students work in "teams." Team one reads aloud, and then the team two reads aloud the same section. Team two continues on to the next section, followed by team one echoing the selection.
Whole class echo reading with varied interpretations and discussion	The teacher reads aloud, demonstrating correct fluency, and the class repeats aloud, trying to mimic the teacher's pacing and expression.

Vocabulary Activities

Activity	Description
Call and response	The teacher, or another student, provides clues about a word, a definition, or a sample sentence with a synonym, and the students in small groups decide which word the teacher is referring to.

Cards on head	A student holds a card containing a new word on his or her head, without looking at it. The partner tries to define or explain the word sufficiently for the first student to guess the word. Then they switch roles.
Contrast / argument responses	Students take a pro or con position on a statement by the teacher and write a rationale for their position. Students use the new words in their written rationale.
Create-a-dictionary	Students create their own dictionaries of words, including definitions and connotations, word parts, and sample uses. (A graphic organizer is a great way to organize information for a dictionary entry.)
Creating word categories	Small groups categorize words by a variety of criteria, such as parts of speech, synonyms, context, or topic.
Definition mapping	Students fill in definitions in text when they encounter words being studied.
Discussion	During discussion, the teacher asks questions that enable students to use new words, and encourages students to use them when appropriate.
Erase and replace	A form of word swapping, students strike out new words from text and replace them with familiar words or definitions.
Graphic organizers	Using a variety of graphic organizers, such as bubble graphs, students break words into letter–sound combinations, include definitions and uses of the word, and similes and antonyms. (This exact exercise works for phonics, too.)
Identifying context clues	Students study the text surrounding unfamiliar words to identify common phrases, messages, and general sense of a paragraph's meaning or purpose.

Journaling	When writing in their reading journals, students use identified new words that are used in the text.
New word search	Students look through text to find specific vocabulary words and study how they are used; students look through text they are about to read to find unfamiliar words, which they study before reading the text.
Opinion essays	Through discussion, students form an opinion on a topic and write an explanation and rationale for their opinion. Students use the new words in their written opinions.
Partner graphic organizers	Partners or small groups complete a graphic organizer of information about a new word, with sample uses, root words, etc
Response to prompts	Students write short answers to the teacher's prompts or questions. The teacher develops the questions carefully to ensure that the targeted words can be used in the responses.
Visual representation	Students draw a picture that represents the word definition.
Word mapping	Small groups create a graphic organizer or matched lists of words that have similar meanings.

Comprehension Activities

Activity	Description
Book/story review	Students in small groups plan a review and then individual students write a review, which they share with the group.

Cause and effect charts	In small groups, students make a chart that describes a character's actions and the outcome, or an if-then chart with a potential action and likely outcome.
Comic strip	Students create a comic strip to present significant events in a story.
Completing stories	Students write their own endings to stories. This should follow discussion and small-group graphic organizers.
Creating questions	Students develop questions about a text that they will pose during discussion or for other students to answer in short responses.
Discussion board / forum	An asynchronous form of discussion in which students post questions and responses on a board or other type of forum. Students do this throughout reading a text, with responses and answers used as part of discussion.
Gallery / book walks	Small groups prepare posters for books or other visual representations, and then groups browse each other's posters.
Group brainstorming and decision making	Small groups generate ideas and information related to a prompt and seek agreement on the response or interpretation. This may be a form of KWL chart or other process for gathering information, making decisions about the information, and reaching consensus. (The nominal group technique is one good way to do this.)
Group-generated choral read	A small group of students creates a summary of a text or writes a response to a prompt, and then reads it chorally to the class.

KWL chart	A chart for describing what the student KNOWS, WANTS to know, and has LEARNED. Students should modify their KWL charts as they read more.
Paraphrasing	The students restate the major information or central content in writing either to present (e.g., choral read, book poster) or to share during discussion.
Plot lines	Small groups create a timeline of the major points in a story, identifying components of the plot (e.g., setting, rising action, climax).
Posing research questions to other student groups	Small groups create questions for other groups to research and answer. A KWL chart is a good way to develop the questions. If used with non-fiction text, research may include a variety of sources.
Promotional posters	In preparation for a book walk (or in place of other forms of text summaries), students create book promotional posters that not only represent the main themes or content but also express what is interesting or compelling about the text. (One of the few arts-and-crafts type projects I espouse.)
Read-respond-share	A general type of activity in which students read a text, respond to a prompt or questions, and share their responses and justifications with a small group. Each small group of students should have one or two prompts / questions, and other groups may have different questions. The discussion addresses all questions.
Reflection journal	Students write freely about a text they have read or are reading. On occasion, the teacher may provide prompts.

	These are not ever graded, but the teacher may collect them from time to time and provide comments. Their main purpose is to help students reflect on their ideas.
Research questions	See "posing research questions to other students groups."
Response to higher-level questions	This is a fundamental aspect of small group discussion, and prompts and other activities can include questions that address higher levels of Bloom's Taxonomy.
Semantic maps	A map of word usage in a text, similar to a graphic organizer for vocabulary, but focusing on word interpretation as used in the text.
Snowball discussion	Students in a small group call on one another to add information or additional responses to the questions.
Sticky notes	Two ways to use sticky notes: 1) mark important information in the text, in which case the student leaves himself or herself a note about the content, meaning, or value, action; 2) create a very short summary of a paragraph or important section in the text, in which the size of the sticky notes forces students to be concise and focus on the main point.
Structured debate	In 2 pairs, students argue for their particular interpretation of the text using standard formal debate rules. This can take quite a bit of preparation time but can produce amazing information.
T-chart for questions and answers	Students create a t-chart with questions on one side and answers, as they discover them, on the other.

T-chart for comparison	Students create a t-chart of comparable topics on either side, such as character comparisons, biases, points of view, their own and other students' interpretations. Many options.
Thumbs up / thumbs down	A very fast self-check on comprehension. The teacher stops the students during an oral reading, SSR, etc. and asks for thumbs up or thumbs down. Two thumbs up for good comprehension, two down for no comprehension, or one of each for tentative understanding. This indicates to the teacher whether or not to stop for discussion about the text.
Timelines	Students use a timeline to describe the order of events, steps, ideas, etc.
Venn diagrams	Students use a Venn diagram to compare and contrast two topics, ideas, characters, points of view, etc.

Appendix B
Sample Lesson Plans

The sample lesson plans on the following pages are intended to demonstrate how you can incorporate all six reading components into single lessons. Each lesson is intended to last about an hour.

If the content, rigor, reading skill, and anticipated learning results are appropriate for your students, you can try them in your classroom. Regardless, as you review them, reflect on how they

- address the reading components,
- engage students,
- implement instructional principles,
- promote discussion, and
- use meaningful texts as the basis for a variety of activities.

Also, consider how they are similar or different to the lessons you provide and think about how you can use a similar approach in your classroom.

K–1 Grade: Green Eggs and Ham

Overview

This lesson uses Dr. Seuss's book *Green Eggs and Ham* to play with words; discuss beginning, middle, and end of a story; and discuss the concepts of stubbornness, persistence, and acceptance.

Materials

Copies of the book *Green Eggs and Ham*, small cards or sticky notes that each have 1 of the 50 words in this book: (a, am, and, anywhere, are, be, boat, box, car, could, dark, do, eat, eggs, fox, goat, good, green, ham, here, house, I, if, in, let, like, may, me, mouse, not, on, or, rain, Sam, say, see, so, thank, that, the, them, there, they, train, tree, try, will, with, would, and you), chart paper & markers/crayons). Optional: A scrambled egg turned green with food coloring.

Lesson-Specific Vocabulary

> Double vowel study: boat, goat, rain, good, mouse, house, train, tree, would, could
>
> Short vowel study: am, and, box, fox, ham, let, thank, that
>
> Rhyming: Sam, ham, boat, goat, box, fox,
>
> Compound words: anywhere

Preparation

Place the materials on a table to engage students' interest.

Conducting the Lesson

Step	Description	Reading Components
1	Place students in small groups of 2–4 and have them take turns with each other and tell what they know about eggs and ham. Encourage them as a group to draw pictures or write words on blank pieces of paper.	Oral language development

2	Give the groups 8–10 of the word cards and ask them to place them in 2 or more groups any way they would like, but they need a reason and will have to explain how they sorted the words. (This step allows you differentiate and scaffold based on your students' reading level.)	Phonics, Phonemic awareness, Oral language development, Comprehension
3	Give groups a chance to explain their reasons (e.g., by first letter, number of letters, words known or unknown).	Oral language development, Comprehension, Phonemic awareness
4	Read the book orally to the class. As a group, chorally re-read pages/sections of interest. Then create smaller groups (for example, just the boys, those wearing tennis shoes, those with green on) and have them read sections orally.	Fluency
5	On the board create three columns labeled Beginning, Middle, End. As a group, discuss what happened at these different points in the story and have students come up and write or draw their ideas. Write the words stubbornness, persistence, and acceptance on the board and discuss where in the columns they could go.	Vocabulary, Comprehension, Oral language development
6	Let students work in pairs to make rhymes about food they do or do not like to eat. Give examples and then let them write and read their own.	Phonemic awareness, Phonics, Fluency

7	Close the lesson by having students go back to the paper they wrote/drew on at the beginning of the lesson and add things they've learned. You can place the papers on the wall and end with a "Museum Walk" showcasing their work.	Comprehension, Oral language development

Possible Discussion Questions

Questions	Bloom's Level / DOK Level
Are eggs normally green? What is happening on this page?	Remember / Recall & Reproduction
How does Sam try to convince him to eat his eggs? What are some words that describe a person like Sam?	Understand / Recall & Reproduction
How many different types of punctuation are there in the story. Can you explain why they have been used? Why does Sam want him to eat the green eggs and ham?	Apply, Analyze / Skill & Concept, Strategic Thinking
How could you encourage people to eat green eggs?	Analyze / Strategic Thinking
How did the grumpy grouch feel during the story? Why do you think that?	Evaluate / Extended Thinking
Can you retell the story from the point-of-view from Sam-I-Am?	Create / Extended Thinking

2nd–3rd Grade: *Magic Tree House* Series

Overview

This lesson can be easily adapted for any of the *Magic Tree House* books by Mary Pope Osborne, and/or the Fact Tracker books that accompany them. This lesson is created for *Dinosaurs Before Dark*, book 1 of 55.

Materials

Magic Tree House book *Dinosaurs Before Dark*, plastic toy dinosaurs, pictures, and other books about dinosaurs and volcanoes.

Lesson-Specific Vocabulary

Syllabification: prehistoric, triceratops, herbivore, carnivore, magnolia, volcano

Silent letters: pteranodon, kneeled, climb

Endings: nests, flapped, stampeded, teetered, engraved, whistling

R-controlled vowels: dark, anatosaurus, herbivore, carnivore, dinosaur

Preparation

Place the materials on a table to engage students' interest.

Conducting the Lesson

Step	Description	Reading Components
1	Have students choose a dinosaur they would like to be today and have them share why they chose that specific one.	Oral language development
2	Write some of the words they used in their discussion (and/or some from the vocabulary list) on the board and as a group practice decoding, reading them orally, and talking about the meaning.	Phonemic awareness, Phonics, Vocabulary

3	Show students the book and have them make predictions on what they think the book will be like. Write these predictions down for all students to see	Oral language development, Comprehension
4	Begin reading the book to the students. Have them echo read sections, repeating key sections as a group.	Fluency, Phonics
5	Stop periodically in the book to have students summarize and rephrase what is happening in the story.	Comprehension, Oral language development, Vocabulary
6	Ask questions, scaffolding the complexity, to differentiate for your students.	Comprehension, Oral language development, Vocabulary
7	Close the lesson by revisiting and discussing the students' predictions. Finally, let them choose and share with a partner or small group another toy dinosaur to show how they feel at the end of the lesson.	Comprehension, Oral language development

Possible Discussion Questions

Questions	Bloom's Level / DOK Level
Where do Jack and Annie live? What did Jack and Annie use to climb into the tree house?	Remember / Recall & Reproduction
Why didn't Jack want to go into the tree house at first?	Understand / Recall & Reproduction

Who is older, Jack or Annie and how do you know?	Apply, Analyze / Skill & Concept, Strategic Thinking
How did Annie help save Jack's life?	Analyze / Strategic Thinking
What would you have done to help Jack? What parts of the story are real and what parts are fantasy?	Evaluate / Extended Thinking
What might have happened if the tree house hadn't taken them home?	Create / Extended Thinking

3rd–4th Grade: Spiderman Comics

Overview

This lesson uses Spiderman comics to engage students with reading in a graphic format. The lesson can easily be adapted to any comic book.

Materials

A variety of Spiderman comic books (from easy reading level to harder), paper and writing tools

Lesson-Specific Vocabulary

    Sounding out: stamina, strength, intellect, armor

    Blends: venue, victory, opponent, synchronized, referee, alpine, podium

    Segmentation: ambush, multitude, defend

    Soft c and g: genius, gadgets

    Silent letters: fighter

    Double vowels: villain, genius, speed, recruit, companion, foes

    Endings: terrifying, allies

Preparation

Place the materials on a table to engage students' interest.

Conducting the Lesson

Step	Description	Reading Components
1	Write sentences on the board: "With great power comes great responsibility." "Be who you are." "Do good things even if you don't get the credit." Divide students into three groups. Each group discusses what they think it means and reports to the class.	Oral language development, Comprehension

2	Have students quickly look through a comic book and in two minutes make a list of the hardest words they find or words they think their classmates won't know. (They can't choose characters' names). Take the words noted the most often and discuss the meanings.	Phonics, Vocabulary
3	Take words from students' lists and/or vocabulary lists to model and discuss sounding out, adding and deleting sounds, blending, segmenting, double vowel words, or other skills needed.	Phonemic awareness, Phonics, Vocabulary
4	Pair up students (strong reader and a lower one). Have them read aloud chorally. Then let them reread the story by parts, either by character or by scene. Rotate from group to group to help with pronunciation and pacing and to ask probing questions that will be used in the class discussion.	Fluency, Phonics, Oral language development, Comprehension
5	Have the pairs draw and write a new scene that would fit into the story.	Vocabulary, Phonics, Comprehension
6	Join 2 groups together to read and share their new scene and to explain why they decided upon that particular scene and wording.	Oral language development
7	Return to the three sentences and lead a discussion with students. Students should give examples from what they read that would related to each of the sentences. Have them write and share their opinion on their favorite phrase.	Oral language development, Vocabulary, Comprehension

Possible Discussion Questions

Questions	Bloom's Level / DOK Level
Where is this story taking place? Who are the key characters?	Remember / Recall & Reproduction
What problem is Spiderman trying to solve? Who do you think the villain is?	Understand / Recall & Reproduction
What question would you ask of Spiderman? What choices does he face?	Apply, Analyze / Skill & Concept, Strategic Thinking
What was the turning point in the story?	Analyze / Strategic Thinking
Do you think Spiderman should be allowed to fight crime? Why?	Evaluate / Extended Thinking

4th–5th Grade: Go for the Gold Series

Overview

This lesson uses the Winter 2018 Olympics to engage students to imitate what Olympic-caliber athletes do over and over: prepare, practice, and perform.

Materials

White board and markers for each student; collection of Olympic pictures; library books about Olympic athletes; sports items; and anything else Olympic related you have available

Lesson-Specific Vocabulary Concepts

> Syllabication: contestant, nationality, participant, preliminary, spectator, stamina, sportsmanship, endurance, competitor
>
> Homophones/homonyms: sponsor, vault, defeat, substitute, tire, jump
>
> Blends/vowel study: venue, victory, opponent, synchronized, referee, alpine, podium
>
> Rhyming: medal, standing, Nordic
>
> Compound words: underdog, freestyle

Preparation

Place the materials on a table to engage students' interest.

Conducting the Lesson

Step	Description	Reading Components
1	Group students by twos or threes. Ask students to choose an item and explain to their partner or group why they chose it. Listen in while they are explaining and make sure everyone gets a chance to speak.	Oral language development

2	Give students a white board and marker. For two minutes, students write or draw everything that comes to mind when they hear the word "Olympics."	Comprehension Vocabulary
3	Have all students put their white boards down and do a gallery walk. They will look at their peers' work, read what other students wrote, and find something to compliment about it. If there are questions, the student who wrote on the white board will answer. (This is where the teacher looks and listens closely at the vocabulary use and spelling that can be embedded throughout the lesson.)	Oral language development, Comprehension Vocabulary
4	Explain that all Olympic athletes must prepare, practice, and perform. Although you won't be asking them to figure skate today, at the end of this lesson they will be performing, so preparation and practice must come first. Explain that they are going to create and read some Olympic onomatopoeic couplets for their performance.	Comprehension, Vocabulary
5	Write "onomatopoeia" and "onomatopoeic" on the board and discuss what they mean and how to pronounce them. Have students practice chorally saying the words. Guide students through brainstorming examples (e.g., bees that buzz, clicking of the keyboard, baby's burp). List examples associated with the Olympics (e.g., zoom, swish, bang, clap, bump, clatter, cough). Echo read the words and discuss meanings.	Vocabulary, Phonics, Phonemic awareness, Oral language development

6	As a class, create two-line rhyming couplets using some of the words you have been studying. Write the couplets for all to see on the board, and have students write on their whiteboards.	Phonemic awareness, Phonics, Vocabulary
	Example: Out of the starting gates with a swish and a zoom, / The ski jumper lands but a fall gives him gloom. / The clouds rumbled and the winds gave a hiss, / But the skiers, no gates did they miss.	
7	As a group, practice choral reading the couplets. Then have students practice echo reading. Finally, have each student perform a reading out loud for the group. Discuss what kind of simple scoring system could be created (pronunciation, tempo, loudness, style) and have students rate each other.	Fluency, Phonics, Oral language development, Vocabulary
8	Summarize the main events of the lesson, asking students to share what they prepared, practiced, and performed. End with a round of applause for all the reading athletes.	Oral language development, Comprehension

Possible Discussion Questions

Questions	Bloom's Level / DOK Level
What do you already know about the Olympics?	Remember / Recall & Reproduction
What are the similarities and differences between winter and summer Olympics?	Understand / Recall & Reproduction

What are the differences and similarities between a snow boarder and a skier?	Apply, Analyze / Skill & Concept, Strategic Thinking
What are the benefits of practice for Olympic athletes?	Analyze / Strategic Thinking
Who do you consider to be the best athlete from the USA going to the Olympics? Why?	Evaluate / Extended Thinking
What is a new winter sport you would like to try?	Create / Extended Thinking

4th–5th Grade: *Island of the Blue Dolphins*

Overview

This lesson introduces students to the book Island of the Blue Dolphins and sets the stage for more in-depth coverage of the topics of adversity, hardship, and courage.

Materials

Copies of the novel (preferably one for every 2 students); map of the coast of California; collection of small pebbles, rock, and feathers; pad of sticky notes; paper and writing tools

Lesson-Specific Vocabulary

Syllabication: forlorn, beckon, cormorant, adversity, hardship

Homophones/homonyms: awl, prey, haul, rite

Vowel study: parley, mesa, ravine, intruder, befall, surge, abound, portion, decree, ponder, lair, league

Consonant study: carcass, scurry, gorge, nettle, concealed, ceasing

Preparation

Place the materials on a table to engage students' interest.

Conducting the Lesson

Step	Description	Reading Components
1	Have each student take one of the small items and write a simile or a metaphor about the item on a slip of paper. Provide some examples from the story.	Oral language development, Comprehension
2	Take 4–5 slips to show on a document camera and have the class chorally read them. Discuss whether the samples are metaphors or similes.	Fluency, Oral language development

3	Divide the class into three groups and ask each group to define one of these words: "courage," "adversity," or "hardship." Students use the word discovery process to create working definitions or they can discuss the words in their groups to come up with their own definitions. Have each group member then get with one other member from the other 2 groups and read them their definition.	Oral language development, Comprehension
4	Group students into pairs. Each pair should "whisper read" the first chapter (about 15 minutes) together. Move about the room to help with correct pronunciation and pacing. Have the students read a sample to you. Give each student some sticky notes, and as they come across a word they can't read or don't know the meaning of, have then write it on a sticky note.	Fluency, Vocabulary, Phonics
5	Take words from the sticky notes or the vocabulary list and spend 10–15 minutes on word study with graphic organizer, focusing in on the skills suggested above or on one your students' needs. Have students write down the words as you discuss them to reflect upon later.	Vocabulary, Phonics, Phonemic awareness, Oral language development
6	Have each student write a 2–5-sentence opinion whether they would like to continue reading the book or not. As a class, discuss students' opinions. If the general consensus is to continue reading, have students find a new partner and repeat steps 4 and 5.	Comprehension, Oral language development

Possible Discussion Questions

Questions	Bloom's Level / DOK Level
Where is the setting of this story? What characters are introduced in the first chapter?	Remember / Recall & Reproduction
What point of view does the author use? How do you know? Why did Karana continue to dig roots as the Aleut ship approached?	Understand / Recall & Reproduction
How do we learn about Karana's character? What words describe the environment?	Apply, Analyze / Skill & Concept, Strategic Thinking
Describe a time when you or someone you know were courageous or overcame a hardship. Did you or this person change as a result? How?	Analyze / Strategic Thinking
What feelings does Karana have in the first chapter? Describe a time you had those feelings. Do you prefer male or female lead characters? Why?	Evaluate / Extended Thinking
If you wrote this chapter from the third person point of view, how would it change? Why?	Create / Extended Thinking

6th–7th Grade: Weather Maps

Overview

This lesson focuses on technical reading of weather maps and then pairs students to create and present a weather forecast for the class.

Materials

Collection of different weather maps cuts from newspapers; reference books/Internet sites on weather and weather forecasting; vocabulary words individually written on slips of paper; Paper and writing tools.

Lesson-Specific Vocabulary

> Etymology: istotach, isotherm, cyclonic, millibar
>
> Prefixes/suffixes: meteorologist, ascend, descend, anticyclonic, radiosonde, isobars, reflectivity, precipitation
>
> Double consonants: satellite, scattering, Doppler effect, occluded
>
> Other terms: radar, Coriolis effect, counterclockwise, monitor

Preparation

Place the materials on a table to engage students' interest.

Conducting the Lesson

Step	Description	Reading Components
1	Set a timer for 2 minutes and have each student create his or her own mind map/concept map of what they know about forecasting the weather. Have students find a classmate to compare their maps.	Oral language development, Comprehension
2	Ask students whether they have any questions about forecasting the weather, and have students write their questions on the board.	Oral language development, Vocabulary

3	Create pairs of students. Give each pair one of the weather maps and have them read the symbols. They should decide what the symbols mean and what the forecast would be for a certain location on the map.	Phonics Vocabulary Comprehension
4	Give each pair a few of the vocabulary words to use and have them use the resources to find the meaning. Have them use one of your weather maps and see how those words relate to the maps.	Comprehension, Vocabulary
5	As a whole group, discuss and practice the correct enunciation of the words, the etymology, and other phonics skills as needed.	Vocabulary, Phonics, Phonemic awareness
6	Have the students write out a weather forecast that could be used in a TV segment of the news.	Oral language development, Vocabulary
7	Have students find another pair. Each pair should practice reading out loud their forecast and offer constructive tips the other team's presentation.	Fluency, Oral language development, Comprehension
8	Have pairs present their final weather forecast either to the larger group or to half of the class.	Fluency, Oral language development
9	Have each student take his/her initial concept map and add any new information or vocabulary. Finally, students write an opinion about whether or not they would consider a career in weather forecasting.	Comprehension, Vocabulary

Possible Discussion Questions

Questions	Bloom's Level / DOK Level
What do you know about weather forecasting? How do we decide what the weather is going to be?	Remember / Recall & Reproduction
What folklore tales do you know about the weather?	Understand / Recall & Reproduction
How do weather balloons and radar help us gather information for weather forecasts?	Apply, Analyze / Skill & Concept, Strategic Thinking
Who needs good weather forecasts and why?	Analyze / Strategic Thinking
How could climate change affect weather patterns? What part of weather forecasting would you consider studying and learning more about? Why?	Evaluate / Extended Thinking
What is your opinion of our local weather forecasting? What would happen if we never had access to any more weather reports?	Create / Extended Thinking

Appendix C
Suggested Readings

Bloom's Taxonomy (n.a.). "Bloom's Taxonomy questions". http://www.bloomstaxonomy.org/Blooms%20Taxonomy%20questions.pdf

Brooke, E. (n.a.). "The critical role of oral language in reading instruction and assessment". Lexia Learning. https://www.lexialearning.com/resources/white-papers/oral-language

Butler, S., Urrutia, K., Buenger, A. et al. (2010). "A review of the current research on vocabulary instruction". National Reading Technical Assistance Center. https://www2.ed.gov/programs/readingfirst/support/rmcfinal1.pdf

Butler, S., Urrutia, K., Buenger, A.. & Hunt, M. (2010). "A review of the current research on comprehension instruction". National Reading Technical Assistance Center. https://www2.ed.gov/programs/readingfirst/support/compfinal.pdf

Center on Teaching and Learning, (n.a.). "Big ideas in beginning reading: Phonemic awareness". University of Oregon College of Education. http://reading.uoregon.edu/big_ideas/pa/pa_sequence.php

Commission on Reading of the National Council of Teachers of English. (2004). "On reading, learning to read, and effective reading instruction: An overview of what we know and how we know it". Author. http://www2.ncte.org/statement/onreading/

Connecticut State Department of Education. (n.a.). "Instructional strategies that facilitate learning across content areas".Author. http://www.sde.ct.gov/sde/lib/sde/pdf/curriculum/section7.pdf

Dahlgren, M. (2008) Oral language and vocabulary development: Kindergarten and first grade (Presentation slides from the Reading First National Conference). https://www2.ed.gov/programs/readingfirst/2008conferences/language.pdf

Dahlitz, M. (2016). "The triune brain". The Neuroscience of Psychotherapy Magazine. http://www.neuropsychotherapist.com/the-triune-brain/

Francis, E. (n.a.). "What exactly is Depth of Knowledge? (Hint: It's not a wheel!)" ASCD. http://edge.ascd.org/blogpost/what-exactly-is-depth-of-knowledge-hint-its-not-a-wheel

Gould Boardman, A., Roberts, G., Vaughn, S., et al. (2008). "Effective instruction for adolescent struggling readers". Center on Education. https://wvde.state.wv.us/titlei/documents/AdolStrugglingReadersPracticeBrief.pdf

Herron, J. (2008). "Why phonics teaching must change". Educational Leadership. ASCD. http://www.ascd.org/publications/educational-leadership/sept08/vol66/num01/Why-Phonics-Teaching-Must-Change.aspx

Hess, K. (2004). "Applying Webb's Depth-of-Knowledge (DOK) levels in reading". National Center for Assessment. https://www.nciea.org/sites/default/files/publications/DOKreading_KH08.pdf

Hudson, F., Lane, H. & Pullen, P. (2005). "Reading fluency assessment and instruction: What, why, and how?" Florida Center for Reading Research. http://www.fcrr.org/publications/publicationspdffiles/hudson_lane_pullen_readingfluency_2005.pdf

Marzano, R. (2000). "Ten effective research-based instructional strategies" in R. Marzano What works in classroom instruction. ASCD. http://web.nmsu.edu/~susanbro/sc2/docs/research_based_strategies.pdf

McLeod, S. A. (2012). "Zone of proximal development". Simply Psychology. https://www.simplypsychology.org/Zone-of-Proximal-Development.html

Moats, L., & Tolman, C. (2009). "The development of phonological skills" in Moats & Tolman Language essentials for teachers of reading and spelling (LETRS). Sopris West. http://www.readingrockets.org/article/development-phonological-skills

National Reading Panel. (2000). "Reports of the subgroups. Teaching children to read: An evidence-based assessment of the scientific research literature on reading and its implications for reading instruction". U.S. Department of Health and Human Services, National Institute of Child Health and Human Development. https://www.nichd.nih.gov/publications/pubs/nrp/Documents/report.pdf

National Reading Panel. (2000). "Teaching children to read: An evidence-based assessment of the scientific research literature on reading and its implications for reading instruction". U.S. Department of Health and Human Services, National Institute of Child Health and Human Development. https://www.nichd.nih.gov/publications/pubs/nrp/Pages/smallbook.aspx

NICHD Early Child Care Research Network. (2005). "Pathways to reading: The role of oral language development in the transition to reading". American Psychological Association. http://psychology.cas2.lehigh.edu/sites/psychology.cas2.lehigh.edu/files/pathway_to_reading.pdf

Oregon Department of Education (n.a.). "Depth of Knowledge (DOK) overview chart". Author. http://www.ode.state.or.us/teachlearn/subjects/socialscience/standards/depthofknowledgechart.pdf

Rasinski, T. (2004). "Creating fluent readers". Educational Leadership. ASCD. http://www.ascd.org/publications/educational-leadership/mar04/vol61/num06/Creating-Fluent-Readers.aspx

Rauth, J. & Stuart, R. (2008). "Sound instruction: Phonemic awareness in kindergarten and first grade" (Presentation slides from the 5th annual National Reading First Conference). http://reading.uoregon.edu/big_ideas/pa/pa_sequence.php

Reading First in Virginia. (n.a.). "Reading First: A guide to comprehension instruction". University of Virginia. http://www.readingfirst.virginia.edu/prof_dev/comprehension/introduction.html

Rosenshine. B. (2012, spring). "Principles of instruction: Research-based strategies that all teachers should know". American Educator. https://www.aft.org/sites/default/files/periodicals/Rosenshine.pdf

Semrud-Clikeman, M. (n.a.) "Research in brain function and learning". American Psychological Association. http://www.apa.org/education/k12/brain-function.aspx

Sweeny, S. & Mason, P. (2015). "Research-based practices in vocabulary instruction: An anlysis of what works in grades prek–12". Massachusetts Reading Association. https://www.massreading.org/wp-content/uploads/2015/08/vocabulary-paper-newletterhead.pdf

Sweet, P. (2000). "Ten proven principles for teaching reading". National Education Association. http://www.nea.org/assets/docs/HE/mf_10proven.pdf

Willis, J. (2014). "The neuroscience behind stress and learning". Edutopia. https://www.edutopia.org/blog/neuroscience-behind-stress-and-learning-judy-willis

For information about professional development options, please contact

David Bowman
david@RIRoadmap.com

www.ingramcontent.com/pod-product-compliance
Lightning Source LLC
Chambersburg PA
CBHW071710090426
42738CB00009B/1728